Hunting the Comeback Trail
Revised

Hunting the Comeback Trail
Revised

by Bill Padilla

DORRANCE PUBLISHING CO., INC.
PITTSBURGH, PENNSYLVANIA 15222

All Rights Reserved
Copyright © 2008 by Bill Padilla
No part of this book may be reproduced or transmitted
in any form or by any means, electronic or mechanical,
including photocopying, recording, or by any information
storage and retrieval system without permission in
writing from the publisher.

ISBN: 978-0-8059-7777-6

Printed in the United States of America

First Printing

For more information or to order additional books,
please contact:
Dorrance Publishing Co., Inc.
701 Smithfield Street
Third Floor
Pittsburgh, Pennsylvania 15222
U.S.A.
1-800-788-7654
www.dorrancebookstore.com

Acknowledgments

I can't express the number of people that have helped me through my recovery. My parents, friends, relatives, The NRA, Foundation for North American Wild Sheep, Safari Club International, The Disabled American Veterans, Ducks Unlimited, Laramie County Community College, The University of Wyoming, selected personnel of The Cheyenne Veteran's Administration, selected members of Fitzsimons Army Medical Center, Outdoor Buddies, Hell-of-a-Hunt of Wyoming, The American Legion, Dorrance Publishing, all the outfitters I have hunted with and contacted for information, Craig Boddington, Jim Zumbo, Senator Malcolm Wallop (R-WY), Bayless, Barrett, attys. at law, Mind menders, my ex-wife, Ricki, Al Langston, and many others.

Contents

Introduction v
1. Breaking My Back to Hunt 1
2. Early Hunts 8
3. Birds 13
4. Eye Love to Hunt 15
5. Roy's Ram 26
6. A Little Help From My Friends 31
7. Two Wheel Drive 39
8. Close to My Heart 49
9. Peace of My Mind 60
10. Stoned 80
11. Hunting is Rehabilitation 94
12. Bad Luck Bulls 116
13. Bighorns 122
14. There is Help 132
Afterword 145

Introduction

Hunting the Comeback Trail tells the stories of several hunters that either have disabilities or other health problems; of how they incurred health impairments and continued to hunt despite their handicaps. They didn't let their individual problems interfere with the sport they loved the most— hunting. The desire to hunt again helped drive them through their difficulties and became a release from the limited world they had adjusted to. Severe health problems need not stop individuals from sports that they love. Acceptance, compensation, and adjustment allow all these men to enjoy a sport that they live for.

Jim Hinckley is a totally disabled Ex-Air Force sergeant who has undergone five back operations, four spinal fusions, multiple disc removals, and over a year of hospitalization. Jim has undergone hell, yet still hunts, though not like he once did. He enjoys many of the things that he once took for granted.

Hinckley had been my neighbor when I lived with my parents in Cheyenne, Wyoming before and after my spell in the service. His compassion and savvy were instrumental in my homecoming from Fitzsimons Army Medical Center in 1979. We spent many hours flinging arrows downrange in '79 and '80. The sport was a rehabilitation vehicle for my paralyzed left arm as well as my damaged mind.

Roy Kern hunts better with one eye than most people do with two. The electronics store owner nearly killed himself in high school while skinning a six-point bull elk, losing his left eye. Kern has successfully hunted all types of big game including bighorn sheep with a pistol. He is active in the Laramie Trap Club, shooting clay-birds, competitively.

Pat Clark is a decorated Vietnam veteran who survived the war only to be cut down by an accident a year later. Now, hobbling on crutches, the paraplegic has used army sniper skills to fill nine straight elk tags near Jackson Hole, Wyoming.

Clark hunted elk with me in Jackson Hole during early November of 1992. I met him through a hunting buddy of mine in Cheyenne. I can only admire the sheer guts and determination that allow him to hunt so successfully. A resident of Spearfish, South Dakota, Pat has secured a permit from that state and Wyoming that allows him to hunt from his vehicle. He hunts both deer and elk in this fashion.

Jerry Johnson survived a foolish vehicle accident when he was just 20 years old that left him confined to a wheelchair. Jerry loves the outdoors and is now the head of an organization in Nebraska that helps disabled hunters enjoy their sport.

Ken Hall survived two multiple-bypass heart operations and works for a printing store in Laramie, Wyoming. He went on to successfully hunt trophy bighorn sheep and big elk in Wyoming in addition to many other animals. He didn't let his health problems get in the way of enjoying the sport that he loves and has even guided other hunters to their game in that state.

I spent Christmas of 1978 in a month-long coma. My ability to think and write again took long, hard work and along with hunting, have been vehicles to the level of recovery that I've attained. I was an army lieutenant, stationed in the Northern Bavarian city of Schweinfurt, Federal Republic of Germany. I was making plans to hunt in Germany as well when a tragic vehicle wreck dashed my promising army career.

There are organizations, guide services, special equipment, and special hunts all adapted for the person with an impairment. There is no need to sit around and dream of hunting when there are many ways to do it. All of us are different individuals, but we share some common ground in our love of the hunt and our own struggles. Trial, compensation, and adjustment allow all these men to enjoy a sport that they live for.

Chapter 1
Breaking My Back to Hunt

Sergeant Jim Hinckley and Airman Dial Campbell were assigned to Frances E. Warren Air Force Base in Cheyenne, Wyoming. The pair's military occupation specialty (MOS) was police-dog trainer. One cool November morning in 1974 the two were given the task of constructing new cinder block dog kennels for a new batch of canines coming in from Lackland Air Force Base near San Antonio, Texas. In the military, enlisted men always drove non-commissioned officers and officers around. Campbell was driving a load of cinder blocks while Hinckley rode shotgun.

"Turn the rock-n-roll music down, Dial," complained the shivering junior NCO (non-commissioned officer). "If you can't find a country station, you might as well leave it off."

"Man, how do you get off on that crap?," said the enlisted-man. "They don't play that where you're from in New York."

"Listen Dial; when in Rome...and I really like Wyoming," said Hinckley while dipping snuff. "I love the outdoors, the West, and the lifestyle here."

"Man, you can have it!," shot Campbell, coldly. "Nothing but a bunch of red-necked hicks out here. I can't wait till I'm done with the service."

"You've got to make the best of the situation, Dial," encouraged Hinckley. "If ya don't, it'll drive you crazy. We got the best hunting and fishing in the country out here. This is paradise!"

"Paradise for you and hell for me," challenged Campbell. "I'm not the only airman who thinks so."

Campbell pulled a deuce-and-a half into the area slated for construction on F.E. Warren AFB. Piles of cinderblock lay where the pair had already unloaded the previous truckload. Hinckley climbed into the back of the truck to begin unloading. Jim started pitching blocks off the vehicle with the truck running. Campbell's foot slipped off the clutch pitching the truck violently forward. Jim flew off the rear and into a pile of cinderblocks.

Jim lay writhing in pain atop the pile with four fractured vertebra and multiple ruptured discs.

"Jim!" screeched Campbell. "What have I done?"

Jim moaned instructions to his subordinate.

"Better get a meatwagon. I really screwed my back up, ehh!"

Thoughts of the future ran through Jim. He had a baby boy at home to support along with his wife. Recreation came secondary but Jim couldn't help wondering about his coming hunting trips. Pain rushed through his body.

Dial raced to get a military ambulance after initially giving assistance to Jim. Hinckley was rushed to F.E. Warren Hospital and after initial inspection, flown to Fitzsimons Army Medical Center (FAMC) in Denver, Colorado.

Hinckley would spend much of the next year undergoing treatment, surgery, and therapy at Fitzsimons. He underwent further treatment at FAMC over the next few years. Jim was wheeled onto Five-West Neurosurgery, which was under the direction of Dr. John Slaughter. Some of Five-West's staff had names that would make anyone think about undergoing treatment there. The head nurse was Captain Hook, a Dr. Loveless practiced there, as did Dr. Haight.

Hinckley endured four back operations during this period involving disc removals and spinal fusions. While in a body cast Jim was allowed to socialize at Fitzsimons NCO Club. Jim needed some relief while enduring a three-month body cast while his back healed.

"How 'bout stretching that body cast across a pool table," called Sergeant Fred Turner to Hinckley, himself recovering from back surgery. "We sure need to get off this ward. I came over here last week with a couple other patients."

"I can't stand this ward myself," said Jim, hobbled by his half-torso cast. "The staff'll let us out of there for awhile. They probably would like to see us leave for good."

The duo took the Fitzsimons military taxi to the NCO Club on post, discussing their feelings about Five-West.

"Don't like being up there very much," Jim grimaced trying to get comfortable in the back of the vehicle. "Lots of pain up there and no way to escape from it. I've been up there for months now."

"I haven't been up there like you but I know what you mean," replied Turner. "If everyone had their own room, it wouldn't be so bad."

Five-West was set up as one large ward with curtains dividing the rooms. Privacy wasn't one of the strong points of the floor. But then, that is the way the military is, with privacy being a premium.

Pulling up in front of the NCO Club, the two Air-Force veterans extracted themselves from the taxi and hobbled in. Hinckley arranged a litter to support himself while shooting a game of eight-ball. Waitresses brought a pitcher of beer and two frosty-cold mugs. Fred broke and Jim pulled his litter around the table for each shot, gulping brew down.

Jim and Fred were starting their second game when Jim's litter tangled on a cord and fell. Jim vaulted down a ramp into a table of more NCO's, sending beer flowing everywhere and fracturing his body cast as well.

"You okay, Jim?" Turner wanted to extend a hand but remembered his back was hurt also.

"Doc Slaughter ain't gonna like this," Jim gasped amidst the broken chairs and beer.

The pair rode back to the main hospital in an ambulance. When Jim was examined by Dr. Slaughter back on Five-West, the full colonel was not laughing at the mishap.

"We'll do our best Sergeant," said the medical officer. "But do we have to send babysitters out with all our patients that leave the hospital?"

Jim declined to answer the furious army officer. Hinckley lay more amused by the situation than fearful of the army colonel. He did not display any emotion before the neurosurgeon. Jim was not having much pain after the fall, so he wasn't too worried.

Such trauma would be serious for anyone, though Jim was entertained. However he did realize the seriousness of the situation as he lay before the department head. No damage was incurred in the mishap at the pool table. Dr. Slaughter replaced the body cast while Jim was hung by equipment for the procedure. Jim endured the hospitalization, making him anxious to try hunting again though he would never hunt like he did before. Jim had spent his entire life hunting in upstate New York and had enjoyed hunting in Wyoming.

He was excited to be stationed in a prime outdoor state like Wyoming. Jim had hunted for the experience, camaraderie, unison with nature, etc. Actually killing the animal had dropped in priority, partially because then he had to transport it. Most of the fun was gone after he pulled the trigger. Guiding other hunters excited him now. He could experience the hunt, see the animal, match wits with it, and share in the actual kill. Jim thanked the Lord for success while hunting but more for everything that came along with it.

Jim was plagued by constant pain. He sat with his whole body straight and visibly limped. Lifting weights was forbidden, making him rely on his friends to transport game that he kills. Since he couldn't walk great distances, Jim altered his hunting methods of necessity. He hunted from a stand or lets the game move to him and relied on his sharp vision to do the hunting that his body wouldn't allow him to do.

The disabled veteran was quiet about his back and chose to display his strengths rather than wallow in self-pity. Success in hunting had become secondary or of lesser priority to the veteran now. Part of that attitude was due to his disability, but more a result of growing older and getting more experience under his belt. Jim was very personable and found friends who enjoyed the outdoors with him and helped him wherever he went. The injury made him more attuned to the environment and less judgmental of others.

Back injuries are often unique in that the victims display few external signs of the damage. Because Jim hunts and fishes so actively, many people believe that Jim shouldn't be classified as disabled. Sure, he hunts and fishes but in ways that would drive most individuals crazy.

After his Fitzsimons treatment, Jim was well enough to pursue his love of hunting in 1978. He chose to hunt mule deer with his bow near Cheyenne.

Jim Hinckley proudly sits atop his South Dakota Blackhills bull elk killed in 1993.

Jim doesn't let his back injury slow him down. Here he displays a pair of Blackhills turkey that he took with a friend.

Sometimes sitting in a goose blind is the best therapy you can get, especially when you harvest a handful of Canada geese like Jim has.

Jim guided Roger Freden to this bull elk during 1988 in Wyoming. Roger displays the six-by-six while Jim shoots the picture.

Jim with his 1992 Blackhills bull elk. He relies on his friends to transport his game from the woods. His back will not allow much lifting.

Chapter 2
Early Hunts

After his Fitzsimons treatment, Jim was well enough to pursue his love of hunting in 1978. He chose to hunt mule deer with his bow near Cheyenne.

Finding someone to hunt with is a problem for the disabled. Jim was lucky enough to have his neighbor, a retired fire-fighter from Cheyenne, to share his adventures with. Leo Lish became Hinckley's hunting buddy. The pair hunted out of Hinckley's trailer in nearby Pole Mountain for deer in 1978. Jim couldn't take a lot of walking and neither could the retired fireman.

"You know, if we pattern these deer, Jim, maybe we can set up an ambush for them," said Lish during dinner in the eighteen foot trailer.

"I think we've already done that, Leo," answered the injured hunter. "We just need to pick spots for an ambush when the deer move up and down that ridge. If we're lucky, the deer will be walking and feeding into us like they were browsing yesterday morning."

Jim and Leo set up their ground blinds in an area between the deer's feeding and sleeping areas, waiting for the sun to drop lower. Blind hunting was always a test of patience, no matter what animal is sought. When the sun was already down, four mulies stepped out of their beds and walked slowly down the ridge toward their dinner. The couple nervously watched the mule deer go ambling by just out of range until a young, two-point buck, came right up to Jim. The archer was tense while the young deer came his way. Hinckley sucked snuff while the buck stopped fifty yards away. During his long rehabilitation, Jim had learned patience. Lifting his head, the buck snorted and continued his course right at Jim.

Drawing back his compound bow, Jim lined the pin sights right on the buck's chest. He knew that he couldn't shoot if the animal was watching him so he waited until the buck's head was turned. The buck's ears were moving like radar dishes, seeking any noise that could be threatening. Just as Hinckley was ready to release, the buck stopped behind some pine branches. Holding at full draw, Jim silently thanked the salesman who talked him into a compound bow. It was a lot easier on him. He started to count to himself, slowly, as his back muscles started to strain. After what seemed like an eternity, the buck moved into the clear, head still turned away.

An Easton 2117-grain Gamegetter arrow split the cool evening air and sank deeply into the animal's chest. The buck hunched and then took to the air like a kangaroo until he folded forty yards later. It wasn't a record breaking buck, but he was a trophy to Jim. All the doubts, uncertainties, and ghosts disappeared for awhile and all he saw was a beautiful mule deer buck.

His retired friend helped Jim transport the animal to a road where they could load the deer into their vehicle. Jim was so inspired by the young deer that he had it mounted at Frontier Taxidermy in Cheyenne where he was apprenticing at the time. Leo remained Jim's only hunting-buddy during this period of his recovery. Jim was drawn to older people at this time because of their wisdom, their true feelings, and their reluctance to judge. The pair often looked to the western slope of Snowy Range for many of their hunting adventures. In 1980, the couple scouted an area called Kennady Peak and made their elk hunt in that area that year. Once again, the two hunted out of Jim's trailer at nearby Lincoln Park Campground.

"I don't want to push myself like I have before," said Hinckley to his hunting companion. "I'll sit and watch this waterhole or elk wallow most of the time."

"Yeah, all we need to do is send you back to Fitzsimons," said Leo. "Then what will I do for a hunting buddy."

"I think I've found where my limits are," answered Jim. "It just takes time before you know how hard you can push yourself. The body has its own time frame and pushing it will only set the recovery back."

Jim was a walking fool before his back injury, but that was all in the past. Now, he used more passive forms of hunting. He had found an elk wallow in a slight depression along Fish Creek. Waiting in ambush would be dull and after three days at the elk bath seeing squirrels, birds, and one porcupine, something gave.

The setting sun was hidden by the trees, but the approaching darkness told Jim to be ready. His mind was clear, his attention fixed on the mud hole. A twig snapped to his right and Jim's eyes moved up towards the disturbance. Then another stick popped.

Jim knew that 15 feet was about as close as he wanted to get to a 300 pound black bear. The bruin's nearly combed whiskers moved while the huge male sniffed the pine scented air. At the time, Wyoming's Game and Fish gave elk hunters a bear tag with their elk license. The two predators were eye-to-eye, waiting for some signal from the other. The veteran began to shake out of excitement while beady bruin eyes studied his every shiver. Jim drew first.

Hinckley reached for his compound bow and his sudden move sent the bear into a somersault, clawing for escape. Jim drew quickly and released, striking a young sapling with his arrow. The bear made a quick escape into the thick timber along Fish Creek. Jim panted heavily, fighting the adrenaline pumping through his system. He waited awhile before he returned to camp by flashlight.

"I was about ready to call the sheriff," said Leo, while Jim limped into camp. "Either you were in trouble or you had something down. Now which is it?"

"Neither, Leo, I almost got eaten by a big bear," came Jim's heavy response.

Hinckley related the showdown with the cinnamon-colored bear. Leo wished he had been there as the two planned to do more hunting on Kennady Peak with their bows. Leo suggested that they hunt slowly through a hole that he had found days earlier. The walking wasn't too hard and elk sign was abundant. They drove to the area on the fifth day of their hunt.

Leo entered the depression from the south while Jim took the easy way in, off the road. About 40 minutes into their morning hunt, they heard elk cows chirping from the center of the hole. Jim picked up on the noises, the pair moving like snails into a small herd of talkative elk. The bleat of their talk was all the pair needed to focus upon. The cover was thick but tan elk forms slowly began to appear. Lish moved in closer, getting near the point of drawing his arrow when the herd spooked at the sound of branches breaking.

Jim saw three other hunters moving nosily into the dip, clearly unaware of what was in there. Elk were scattering everywhere while Jim bit his lip against uttering something profane. The noisy hunters never even saw what could have awaited them in the small depression.

The following days were uneventful, but the unsuccessful hunt provided more thrills than many hunters experience in years in the field.

Leo drew a moose tag the following year, 1981. The pair rented horses to hunt the Teton Wilderness, east of Grand Teton National Park. Jim pushed his back too hard on that hunt, and had to retreat to safer, easier hunting methods.

Doctor Roger Freden and son Tom were his guests on a Snowy Range elk hunt in 1988. Jim, the ex-Air Force Sergeant, had hunted the Kennady area so extensively that he was comfortable laying ambush for elk. He knew an area where elk funneled through from above when hunting pressure disturbed them. Roger, however, felt funny waiting for an elk to show up.

"I'd rather be walking for elk, Jim," whispered the elder Freden. "This could get boring. I hope someone will do our work for us."

"That's what we're hoping for," Jim replied. The three of them were waiting for the sky to lighten up. "A lot of elk hunters play this game."

The eastern sky was illuminated by a sunrise that all three were enjoying. When they heard shooting, it put them all on alert. They knew to be quiet at this time of day and in this situation. Sounding like a tractor tearing up the forest, a huge five point bull tore his way through to the forest clearing. Tom and Roger had picked spruce trees as rests before the bull entered the meadow. Roger saw the bull coming, but couldn't find the vital chest area to shoot. His heart racing, Roger glanced at Jim, who gave him the palms-down sign meaning that he didn't have a shot.

Still hidden in the spruce trees, the bull turned enough of his shoulder to present an opening. Roger Freden was open for the shot. He pushed his .30-06 rifle clear of the branches, aimed, breathed in and half-out, and then shot the five point right through the shoulder. Lunging forward, the big five-by-five fell in the small meadow. All three hunters converged on the bull like vultures coming to claim what was theirs. Backslapping and whistles told other hunters of their success. The three hunters cut up the animal and the Fredens transported it back to camp. They reveled in their opening day fortune.

"Good thing you shot, Dad," exclaimed the junior Freden. "Jim was right behind you."

"Actually, I didn't see it over that small hill," Jim confessed. "If Roger couldn't kill him, I don't think any of us could have. You couldn't see too well at your end of the clearing?

"No, but that's why we have guns trained on all ends of that opening," said Tom. "Dad was just the lucky one."

"Yeah, it could have been any of us that killed that bull," said Jim. "Now we have to figure something for tomorrow. I think we ought to stay close to camp."

Jim's strategy for the second day was like the first—sit and wait. Jim thought, *How many hunters stumble through the forest and push game to other hunters?* Sometimes the best plan is to let your eyes do the hunting and not spook game especially when hunting thick timber. Of course, there are many factors involved in a successful hunt.

This time the elk hunting crew decided to deviate from the first plan slightly. Hinckley drove up the road about one-half mile, entering the woods for a haphazard elk drive. Every hunter knows that you don't drive elk, generally. Jim was hoping that a spooked elk would file past Tom. It wasn't time to get tangled in thick underbrush, so Jim stuck to established game trails while moving his way in the direction of the Fredens. The terrain was flat. The veteran was seeing plenty of fresh droppings, tracks, and he inhaled the dank, musky elk scent permeating the pine jungle.

He had no idea what the Fredens were doing over 600 yards away and then it started. The elk sign played with Jim's eyes and nose until he heard branches breaking ahead of him. Trees were being hit with large bodies and branches flew. The sound was unmistakably elk. Jim crouched down, painfully, his eyes scanned the undergrowth. Elk legs were all that he could see, connected to bodies and horns hitting those threes. With no body that he could aim a bullet into, Jim held his breath and waited for the Fredens.

Two shots echoed, followed by Tom yelling for Jim and his Dad. Tom had bagged a mature cow within a few hundred yards of camp.

The trio filled two licenses in two days. Elk hunts are usually long affairs, prompting most hunters to stay at least a week. With two elk in the truck, the party decided to call it a hunt as Jim was getting tired.

Chapter 3
Birds

Jim was retrained as a dental technician in Watertown, South Dakota. Northeast South Dakota is about as good as it gets for pheasant hunting. Jim's in-laws had a farm encompassing hundreds of acres, offering some fine bird hunting. Big game hunters get older and can no longer handle the physical end of the hunt, most turn to bird hunting. They first hunt upland game and then waterfowl when their legs give out.

Jim can't take a full day's walking and many times much less than that. Experience on Bill Rake's farm had taught Jim the right places for birds. When he and his friends trudged the corn fields, Jim blocked or stood motionless as other hunters drove birds his way. Jim took his limitations into account and had found many ways to hunt that put as little strain on his damaged back as possible. As long as the walking wasn't too rough, Jim would step into heavier cover in an attempt to flush birds. Often-times he would use another hunter's dog to flush birds for him. In that way, the dog did all the work while Jim positions himself on a likely escape route for pheasants.

Before Thanksgiving of 1992, Jim entertained one of his hunting friends from Cheyenne. Terry Whitenight arrived in Northeast South Dakota with his German wirehair pointer, a twelve-gauge, and a load of enthusiasm. Whitenight had hunted Central Kansas for several years but cancelled the annual trip to try South Dakota. Terry had hunted birds locally with Jim near Cheyenne and gave assistance to him as needed during a hunt. When Terry arrived at Jim's in-laws' farm, Jim couldn't tell who was more eager for the hunt, Terry or his dog. They started hunting the next day by swinging through the east boundary of the farm. The land was flat and planted with corn. When they crossed a small creek, birds ran for an exit, in every direction. Terry's wirehair went crazy until his master turned him loose. Pheasants took the dog on long chases in all directions. Terry's whistle blasts eventually brought back one excited dog, but not before he had chased a few birds.

"Not one bird held," croaked Terry in his Pennsylvania Dutch drawl. "Maybe I should have waited to come out when there be snow on the ground."

"Yeah, a little snow certainly helps," admitted Hinckley, hands on his hips. "These birds have been hunted pretty hard lately."

But Terry thought, that pheasants had been hunted hard and their numbers weren't down. He drove into many places where the birds exploded everywhere. They did get a few pheasants, but everywhere the pair went, the birds were fleeing as of the two were getting out of the truck. What they needed to do was get a few more hunters involved in the game so they could get the birds surrounded. Jim's phone calls that evening produced a handful of hunters for the big drive. With road running pheasants, often-times the best tactic is a lot of hunters to pursue them. Jim decided to try the system on an adjacent farm since they had spooked more of the birds on Bill Rake's farm that day.

Six hunters arrived in the morning to make the big hunt for running birds. They were shown a field, hunters were given lanes, blockers placed to keep birds from running out of sight, and a whistle blast started the show. It wasn't long into the drive when gaudy sprinters with green or brown heads could be seen, running for the gate.

Terry was driving, or spooking birds, while Jim blocked, at the far end of the field due to his back problem. Dogs weren't used as everyone thought that they would just get in the way. One shot rang when a rooster held long enough to enable one hunter to shoulder his gun for the flush. The birds slowly moved to Jim's end of the field. The action started when game birds began bumping into the blockers at the far end of the field.

Birds began backtracking to try to sneak out the sides, and tried to squeeze between blockers and drivers. Everyone had to be careful and watch their fields of fire. Shots were pumped from all over the field's end. And when it was over, colorful cocks were gathered from the plot. Over the next few days, Jim and Terry put together more schemes for nailing running pheasants. Terry went home with a limit of pheasants and had seen over one thousand birds.

Hinckley got a good feeling out of being able to guide other people to game. He didn't receive payment for this work. His payment is in the self-fulfillment that comes when he leads someone else to success, despite his back problem. Jim will probably experience other types of bird-hunting and perhaps big game. His back is a never ending concern to him but through experience and the help of his friends, he hunts with it.

Chapter 4
Eye Love to Hunt

The spirited 21 year old from Laramie, Wyoming couldn't wait to hunt elk that late October weekend in 1973. Roy Kern had hunted every weekend since the elk season began two weeks earlier. Friday night left an inch of new snow on the ground so Roy knew that any elk sign he found would be fresh. He was hunting with his father, Tom, that Saturday morning atop Centennial Ridge in the nearby Medicine Bow Mountains. Kern liked this area of Snowy Range, having hunted it for years. His father's cabin wasn't far away at the base of the ridge so the pair could warm up as needed.

Snow was lightly falling that morning, but let up as they finished lunch. Roy stepped from his vehicle to hunt some promising country, finding a fresh elk track on a trail that led to a park. Roy followed slowly, knowing that haste is a hunter's worst enemy. Stepping gingerly down the trail, Roy broke into a park where his elk was skirting the perimeter trees as stealthily as he. The mustached hunter had closed the distance to 100 yards from his quarry. The six-point bull looked back over his shoulder. Roy raised his .30-06 rifle and drilled the brute in the neck. Roy didn't break the bull's neck but cut his jugular instead. The bull bled out within 100 yards, leaving a bright red trail for Roy to follow.

Roy and his father cut the elk into three pieces and packed the meat out by 11 P.M. A local taxidermist and personal friend of Roy's persuaded him into mounting the six point bull.

"A lot of hunters go their entire lives and never get a crack at an elk that size," said taxidermist Charlie Thompsen. "You might not get another one."

"I thought about that, Charlie," Roy answered. "Gonna have to pay for it in installments, though."

They quickly hung the elk and broke off until the next morning when Roy pulled the elk into the barn so that he could skin it. Roy had worked as a meat-cutter while in high school so he knew about thawing the elk with an electric heater that morning. He was skinning the right leg on the elk, hoping to get through before dark. With the majority of the processing behind him, he pulled hard on the boning knife to cut through the frozen skin. Suddenly, his knife hit a soft spot that the heater had overthawed. Roy was cutting upward when his knife hit the thaw, thrusting the long dagger into his left eye. The bone of the eye socket stopped the knife from plunging into his brain, saving him. There wasn't much blood. Luckily, a friend was nearby to drive the injured elk hunter to Ivinson Memorial Hospital in Laramie.

At first, Dr. John Carolan tried to save Roy's punctured eye, but after the eye was sewn, Roy experienced failing vision in his good eye. Dr. Carolan opted to remove the damaged eye to save Roy's sight. Roy became protective of his lone eye and bought eyeglasses to shield it even though his vision was better than 20/20. Within two months, he was hunting coyotes in Sybille Canyon near Laramie. Roy had to learn to hunt again with only one eye. Roy and his friend Rusty hunted down a bobcat just as the sun was dropping over the Snowy Range. Roy thumped him at 300 yards with his .220 Swift. He and Rusty found the dead cat with aid of a spotlight though Roy was experiencing night vision better than before. For some reason, the lone eye was taking over for both eyes. Having lost his depth perception, Roy had learned to compensate by estimating. Judging distance, however, was quite difficult for him. Loss of the eye did not deter him from other activities either.

Wanting to become a certified pilot, Roy started taking flying lessons. Without any depth perception, he had a rougher time than most students. Flying took much practice, but Roy eventually developed a feel for it. Roy loved flying because it gave him a feeling of freedom that he had never had. He began scuba diving lessons, and became certified in that sport as well. There wasn't much that Roy would let stand in the way of his normal life. He was enrolled in the state's vocational rehabilitation program. Counselors said that his eye loss didn't affect his work so they paid for some cosmetic work for Roy which would enhance his appearance. He tried racquetball but when Dr. Carolan saw the difficulty that he was having on the court at the local club, he influenced Roy to try another sport. The doctor also informed him that there were a lot of eye accidents caused by racquetball. That was something Roy couldn't afford. Roy returned to big game hunting a year after his accident.

Roy rarely hunted far from his Laramie home, mainly for economic reasons. He chose a nearby mountain for a deer hunt during October of 1974. Sheep Mountain was an imposing, uplift marking the eastern boundary of Snowy Range. Roy hunted it alone that day and was able to drive the mountain. Sheep Mountain was later designated as wilderness with no motor vehicles allowed. However in 1974, a few roads did exist. Roy used one to get him higher on the hill. He parked and began climbing the slope to give him better observation. When he was higher on the hill, he uncased his monocular to get a better look at the opposite slope.

Studying the mountain long and hard revealed two mule deer bucks among its timber. One was worth further inspection. He took out his spotting scope and quickly set it up. Both bucks looked pretty good and one was definitely a keeper. He lined up his .30-06 Springfield and took his time. The deer were totally unaware of the marksman getting ready to fire. He adjusted his rifle hold for the 400 yard distance. Roy had been looking at the bucks for nearly 20 minutes when he decided to fire. He dropped a 150 grain bullet right into the buck's throat. Roy almost never shot at game animals unless it was a head or neck shot. His taxidermist got upset over the repair work he must do to a damaged cape.

Roy crossed the gorge, searching for the dead animal and found the 25 inch buck under a tree. It was nearly a mile back to the truck but Roy carried the buck the entire way. A few stitches would repair the bullet hole.

Roy had always been a successful hunter but after he put his eye out, he felt compelled in his mind, to become even better than before. He and his family rarely ate meat from the store—most of it coming from his hunting forays. In some respects, Roy was a trophy hunter but he felt pressure to put meat on the table as well. Roy did so to master hunting with one eye as well as to prove this to other people. He proudly displayed a box full of elk ivory that he had collected over the years, most within sight of his Laramie home. Roy encountered other problems caused by his eye loss. Roy lost his sense of direction in the woods after his injury. He usually hunted with someone unless he was familiar with the terrain. Sometimes hunting with a buddy was no guarantee that Roy wouldn't get lost. In 1974, Roy and his hunting companion, Al Swain, hunted elk in the central Medicine Bow Mountains. They had hunted the region several times, acquiring a lot of knowledge about game habits in the area over the years. Kern was supposed to search along a road, though remaining back in the trees. Roy naturally veered to his right unless there was some landmark to guide him. He didn't realize how severe his eye condition hindered him until that hunt. He tried to parallel the road, but it was out of sight most of the time. He got confused, made a loop in the trees and came out on a park. Snow was falling heavily by then and dusk was overtaking him. He wanted to go west which would have taken him away from camp and into French Creek, a drainage that was unfamiliar to him.

Across the park he saw another hunter signaling him to walk east toward camp. Roy kept walking, but his confused sense of direction pulled him west again. Once again, Roy saw the same figure waving his arm at him to go east. The same figure must have motioned to Roy over a half-dozen times. Roy wanted to catch up but this specter always remained distant—just close enough to see. Finally, Roy heard a camp generator at about midnight. Roy recognized the camp as one that was close to his. An acquaintance named Dean was in that camp to offer Roy coffee. Roy's first thought was about his partner Al, who was still seven miles away, probably looking for him. Dean gave Roy a ride back up to where he had begun his adventure. They found Swain warming himself in their vehicle, beeping the horn at intervals.

Al chastised Roy as most partners would have.

"Maybe I'll fasten a string to you," lectured Al, hands on his hips. "I've been your friend for more than a few years and I ain't gonna lose you."

"Can't figure that fella that signalled me last night," murmured Roy. "Maybe I do have an angel?"

The next day they slept in. Roy wondered how he'd become disoriented in the forest so he had Al follow him as he hunted through a patch of timber. Al confirmed what Roy had already suspected, that Roy always tended to veer right.

Roy always tried to hunt with someone and he brought maps and a compass along on his hunting trips. He also carried along survival supplies that probably every hunter should carry in the hills. He never did meet the helpful hunter that probably saved his life that night.

In the mid-1970s, Roy killed three bull elk within a quarter mile of each other. Roy did this on his own with his partner Al. Having spent a lifetime in the woods, Roy knew animal behavior especially an elk's. Close to Rob Roy Reservoir in 1975, Roy out thought one nice five-by-five bull by knowing what he would do next.

Roy had learned that elk often use a seesaw pattern of movement of escape always watching their backtrail to detect a pursuer. Roy found fresh tracks in the new snow, and proceeded to follow them. Once on the trail, he immediately recognized the escape pattern and began to wonder, how do I cut this fella off. He would catch glimpses of the bull but he was way out in front of him. Roy thought to cut the seesaw pattern and intercept this bull, hopefully while it was looking back for him. The bull would walk across the timbered hill, then cut back to watch for Kern. Roy hurried quietly, straight uphill. The tactic almost worked, but Roy was a bit late and slightly spooked the bull. Continuing with his jagged pattern, the bull walked faster.

Roy cut uphill, but this time veered to the left hoping to get in front of the animal. Roy's footsteps were masked by the new snow, so he moved quicker. When he broke out on a trail, the elk was only 40 yards away. Roy shouldered his .30-06 slowly and neatly broke the elk's neck. He dressed the bull and returned to camp where he found his excited companion.

"Heard the shot, Roy," clamored Al, his breath clouding from the cold. "One shot's a good sign."

"Yeah, he's laying up the hill," answered Roy, pants sagging at his waist. "We're good for a short pack out, tomorrow."

The next year, provided a lesson in animal and "slob-hunter" behavior. Roy and Al erected their elk camp in the same area as the previous year. When they finished preliminary camp chores, they decided to hunt the same hill as before. They separated with Roy heading back to his place. Slowly moving along a trail, Roy could hear some movement back in the trees. At first he thought it was his friend but then the noises switched to crashing which was too much noise to be Al. Roy was hunting this hill from the top down, as he usually did, when he spied the rag bull at 75 yards through the trees. Roy quickly brought up his rifle and expertly, broke the animal's neck with a bullet. He had mastered hunting before his accident and was now adapting to the sport with just one eye. Al had seen the flash of Roy's .30-06 in the twilight. They finished the chore by dressing the elk with the help of light from Al's cigarette lighter.

They spent over an hour with the bull as Roy wanted it off the ground that night. As they are cutting the bull into pieces, they could hear the footsteps of an animal about 30 yards back in the trees. The sounds kept circling them, and the two wondered what was happening. Roy had regained much confidence after losing his eye but they didn't know what was making the noises so they didn't separate. The two trudged back to their truck for a come-along and flashlight. When they returned, elk tracks circled the dead elk and stepped into Roy and Al's old footprints. Roy thought it amazing that the elk wouldn't leave, even with the human presence. When they got back to camp after hanging the bull, they heard a lone shot in the direction of their elevated bull. The next day, after returning to fetch their bull, they found a gut pile near their quartered elk. Remembering the shot that they heard the night before, they suspected that this elk had been poached. The next year yielded another adventure for the Roy. Roy is a firearm safety instructor in the Laramie area.

Before he taught safety, he had a couple of near fatal mistakes with a firearm. Shortly after the loss of his eye, Roy was playing the gunfighter in a Laramie Jubilee-Days Parade. At the end of the march, a drunken cowboy wanted to see his revolver which was loaded with blanks.

"Mind if I see your weapon?" asked the tipsy cowboy.

"Don't mind if I do," answered Roy, failing to notice the cowboy's condition.

Roy was used to handling a pistol so that a person could grab it by the grips. When this cowboy handled the gun, he accidentally pulled the trigger and shot Roy in the stomach. The blank lodged against Roy's spine, nearly killing him.

Al and Roy hunted together again, spending all morning coursing the pines. At lunchtime, most hunters clear the woods but Roy didn't. He continued to hunt right back to the vehicle. Walking up to a pair of bulls in the spruce, he frightened them but he had his rifle up. He put the cross hairs on the neck of the bigger five-by-six bull at 45 yards and squeezed. The elk didn't fall, just stumbled around, in confusion as to where the shot came from. This enabled Roy to chamber another round for a better shot within 35 yards. But the bull bolted unharmed and left Roy standing stupefied. Roy thought that he couldn't miss a shot that close. The elk were probably headed for Colorado, while Roy stumbled back to camp.

"You didn't drop the rifle or bump your scope?" said Al, sitting perplexed. Roy simply didn't miss shots like those.

"I don't think so, Al," said the electrician.

Roy's self-confidence was badly shaken. He didn't hunt anymore that afternoon, trying to figure out what happened. He began fumbling with his rifle shells, thinking that perhaps the cartridges were bad. Then he noticed the caliber-markings...270 Winchester. That was what Swain was shooting. In the jumble of the camper and the pre-dawn darkness, he must have grabbed Swain's shells. Roy thought himself an extremely lucky man to be unhurt after firing .270-shells from his .30-06.

Roy was back within days to fill his third straight bull tag on a four-point that he had stalked through the timber. After two hours of chase, Roy caught up with the bull along a trail. He raised his .30-06 to drill the male elk through the neck. Always particular about meat handling after the kill, Roy brought the bull back to his truck on his back, in pieces. He had been a meat cutter after school. Roy had similar success with game in the late 1970s.

License firmly in his pocket, Roy chose to hunt his favorite area in 1980. Swain and he pulled into the region after work on a Friday night, established camp, and dozed off in anticipation of the following day. Roy chose to search along Jim Creek on Centennial Ridge, moving slowly as he always hunts. Partially into the hunt, he found elk-cows moving through the trees along Jim Creek. He positioned quickly, waiting for the bull to come through as male-elk usually do, in the rear of the herd. He could catch glimpses of a rag-horn bull herding his females in front of him. He held off until the bull would reveal himself since he had no cow-tag.

When the lead cow was four feet away, she saw Kern standing motionless but ready. The cow pushed through the herd to find the protection of the bull and send the group in a panic towards Roy. Roy's heart was racing at the thought of being trampled by an elk herd. He aimed a shot at the bull's shoulder, connecting. After the close encounter, Roy bolted to follow the bull's trail. He followed the spots of blood in the bull's trail with his one eye—at least the bull was wounded. But he knew that elk can carry a lot of lead before they go down. If the bull was moving that well, he probably would survive the wound.

Once, a fallen animal got his revenge on Roy Kern. Hunting elk again in the same locale, Roy and Al teamed up for a hunt a few years later, in 1984. Roy was getting more confident about hunting in the timber and rarely got lost. He was in the trees when he found a spike bull that wanted to play hide-n-seek in the foliage. This time Al went with Roy, not fully confident about Roy mastering his disability. He, also, wanted to learn how to still-hunt more effectively. They moved slow on the bull. The elk pranced about the fallen limbs, as silent as a ghost.

When they got to within 15 feet of the bull, Roy tried to get his partner to shoot. He pantomimed, signalled, pointed, and mouthed directions to the bewildered Al. The bull was so close that his dank odor filled both men's nostrils. They were both wide eyed as the bull stared them both down. Al finally shrugged and gave Roy the signal to shoot. Roy slowly raised his .30-06 zeroed in on the elk with one eye and hit the bull in the head. There as no rushing up to this elk in that mess of wood and limbs. When they eventually picked their way through to the bull, Roy grabbed him to begin dressing him. The downed-bull stirred and quickly smacked Roy in the face with his hoof, bloodying his nose and sending his glasses flying. Al quickly applied the coup-de-grace to the spike bull as Roy recomposed himself. Roy finished the job after his nose stopped bleeding.

Later that year he killed his biggest antelope buck. Roy had always liked an antelope sector northeast of Rawlins, Wyoming. Antelope area #62 had always harbored a few big bucks. Like everything in the West, it was hammered severely by the killer winter of 1983-84. Severe cold and snow in the spring hammered animals as they were recovering from winter. Finding any large buck was going to be difficult. Roy knew that larger deer and antelope are susceptible to a harsh winter and that deer burn up a lot of body fat during their mating season which falls right before cold weather arrives. Antelope are vulnerable due to their diminutive size and the lack of cover in areas they frequent. The 1983-84 winter devastated big game herds all over the West.

When they hunted antelope that fall, Roy had a feeling that larger bucks just wouldn't be found. Roy's friends filled their quotas one morning on small animals, but antelope were very scarce. The trophy-hunting Roy was the only hunter driving an empty truck. When it became noon, Roy chose to fill out and then return with everyone back to Laramie. Atop a large ridge, Roy spotted a high-horned goat with his monocular. He looked closely for a place to shoot from. His friends had already had an experience with rattlesnakes on this rim. Their gunfire prompted the rattlers to investigate the source of the vibrations. Roy erected a bipod on a rock that he ensured was clear of snakes. He had plenty of time to align the sights and drop a bullet from his .30-06 into the trophy at 600 yards. The buck was smaller than he thought it to be. He had observed that they always seemed to shrink when you arrive at the kill site. Because of the goat's small head, the horns looked massive. They were still over 15 inches long. Roy was rebuilding the confidence he once possessed before his accident.

It wasn't until a few years later that Roy was bit by the trophy hunting bug again. Roy teamed up with a Laramie outfitter, Steve Scheaffer, in 1987 to hunt the sheep country in Montana. Since it was May, they weren't after monster rams. Black bear was their quarry in the Big Thompson country near the Idaho border. This type of country was better suited to hunting after bears rather than baiting or using hounds. The timber was so thick that bears often appeared along the logging roads that dissected the thick forest. One would see grass beside the roads that was mowed by hungry bears, fresh from their winter sleep.

"We'll need some tricks to get them out of that timber," crowed Roy, holding his monocular.

"Hunting bear is exactly that," returned Steve. "They rarely step out of that jungle."

They did much glassing and walking along these roads though they tried to probe the thick, jungle-like forest. Roy's lack of depth perception caused him to stumble several times while negotiating deadfalls. The pair of hunters had decided to split up. When Roy twisted this ankle on one of these logjams, he thought it safer to stay along the road.

Soaking his throbbing ankle in an icy mountain stream when he arrived back at camp, Roy chose to hunt by easier methods. He decided to watch a clear-cut from the top end that evening. Roy's patience had grown as would that of any man who's survived a serious injury. He waited and when shadows started to get long that evening, he spotted his first bear. The black bear was downhill at the bottom of the clear-cut, way out of rifle range. He returned to his earlier method of walking slowly after a short jaunt downhill. There was a road shooting through the trees at the opening's foot which invited Roy.

Roy skirted the trees, keeping hidden in his slow walk down the promising road. When he was around the bend, a brown-colored blackie appeared at 80 yards. Roy wasted no time in getting his .300 Winchester up, aimed at the bear's shoulder, and fired. He didn't want to shoot a bear in the head because that is how the animal is scored. The fine animal needed no finishing shot. Roy stared at the big, cinnamon-colored animal, taking many pictures to remember it by. After Roy had cleaned the bruin and was walking out, he remembered his knife was still at the site of the kill. He quickly backtracked to fetch the blade and found another black bear near the kill site. Roy was sure that this bear was the same one he had spotted from above.

Both men returned the next day to retrieve Roy's trophy and for Steve to track the second bear. When they returned to Wyoming, they each had a six foot bruin in the truck. After that hunt, Roy reached for more challenge and bought himself a hunting pistol for the future. Roy had to test himself by selecting new hunting methods.

In the fall of 1991, Roy returned to his favorite hunting grounds on Centennial Ridge. On his second day of searching the landmark, he spotted a wide-horned monarch uphill near some quaking aspen. Roy followed the animal into the quaking aspen, their yellow and red leaves providing an awesome backdrop to the chase. The thick cover slowed him down so he was relieved when he broke into an open hillside. He sneaked through the shoulder-high brush and stopped occasionally to look ahead. When he stopped the fourth time, he noticed horns sticking up over a rim above him. He couldn't get into a more stable shooting position without losing sight of the buck. He could only see the deer's throat and horns at 80 yards. He had to take an offhand shot at his buck.

He leveled his Thompson Contender hunting handgun, chambered for .30 Herrett. Roy aimed at the buck's head, pulled the trigger and saw him fall. When Roy reached him in the dark, he found the bullet had taken the deer in the head and split the horns. The buck measured 24 inches between the beams and was a typical Western four-point. Roy was fascinated by the animal and the hunt he had give him. He decided to try it again the next year.

The Centennial Ridge mule deer barely missed qualifying for an award from *Handgun International*, so Roy was driven to hunt down a better one. He had to prove, to himself and others, that he was still a superb hunter despite his eye loss. Roy went back to the same ridge and took along his Thompson Contender. Hunting familiar ground, Roy wasn't afraid of getting lost. Good observation and landmarks would identify his position, which was one of the reasons Roy enjoys hunting on this mountain so much. He followed a trail along June Creek on the ridge on his third day of hunting. He looked up on a flat to see two big mule deer looking down on him at 300 yards. This time Roy was able to get into a solid position, handgun resting in a tree fork.

He focused on the bigger mule deer and at that distance he aimed six inches over the buck's head. The deer went right down with a hit in the head. A Roy Kern trademark. This buck was big enough to qualify for *Handgun International* records. Roy used other activities to sharpen his depth perception.

Roy was an avid trap-shooter, serving as an officer in the local trap club. He found that shooting clay birds helped him to judge distance better. He was in the middle of a trap shooting round the next summer when he got notification that he had drawn the king of all Wyoming special permits—bighorn sheep.

Roy Kern with his 1980's mule deer he took near his hometown of Laramie, Wyoming. Kern used a pistol to hammer the four-by-four buck.

Kem hunted Montana's Big Thompson country in 1987 for this black bear.

Chapter 5
Roy's Ram

Bighorn sheep are the pinnacle of big game hunting in North America. Without buying a hunt in Canada or paying exorbitant prices for an auctioned permit in the United States, most hunters have to wait for years before their name is selected in a state lottery for the scarce tags. Roy had waited 26 years before the state drew his tag and when they did, he drew the best sheep area in his home state of Wyoming. Bighorn sheep area number three, south of Cody continually produced the best scoring rams in addition to being the most successful area for sheep in the state.

Roy wanted a different approach to bighorn hunting now that he finally had a tag. His lifetime of hunting, the prime area, self-confidence and a knowledgeable hunting companion convinced Roy to chance it. After waiting decades for a bighorn sheep permit, most hunters would hire an outfitter and a guide. Sheep usually live in remote areas that require much equipment to access. When Roy tried contacting several outfitters for a spartan camp, or drop camp, none would honor his request. Outfitters would rather sell a fully outfitted and guided hunt for the prized trophy.

Ex-Wyoming Game & Fish Warden Bob Sexton of Laramie was eager to accompany Roy for the hunt. Bob taught firearm safety at the National Rifle Association's Whittington Center in Raton, New Mexico during the off-season and had met Wyoming outfitter Ron Dube, there. Ron was constructing a base camp for some bow-hunters who wanted to stalk elk near the area Roy had selected to hunt. Dube agreed to let Bob and Roy hunt from the camp without horses or guides.

Those were tall self-inflicted prerequisites for someone who'd waited decades for a sheep permit. Roy would complicate it further by attempting the hunt with a handgun. His wife Nancy made his Christmas gift of 1992 a custom caliber barrel for the handgun. Roy gleefully unwrapped a .309 JDJ made by gunsmith J.D. Jones of Winterville, Ohio. The .309 JDJ was simply a .444 Marlin case necked down to .30-caliber.

Roy was riding his quarterhorse about one month before his sheep hunt, preparing for September. When he was starting up a ridge, the horse stumbled, then came over backwards pinning Roy underneath. He couldn't walk for some time and cursed his luck so near the start of his dream hunt. The thought of his sheep permit gave him incentive to recover fast. He walked the majority of the 26 miles from Elk Fork Trailhead to Fortress Mountain where Dube's son, Steve, had set up base camp.

Twenty-six miles the elk party, Roy and Bob rode, one for every year Roy had applied for a sheep permit. Each mile was as agonizing as every year he pitted hope against hope, waiting to draw the coveted license. Though retired, Sexton's ride was second nature for the veteran sheep hunter. They arrived the evening before the September 1st opening day.

Instead of a drop-camp, Bob and Roy were allowed to stay at Ron's base camp with all the luxuries of an established outfitter's camp. The only things missing were horses and personal guides and there were bighorns within sight of base camp. Evidence of the 1988 Yellowstone fires were everywhere. Trees were thin in areas while nutritious second growth provided feed for all herbivores. Anxious to hunt, Roy and Bob spent time behind their optics after supper.

"Look at those sheep up there," Bob pointed excitedly, while focusing his Zeiss 10x40 binoculars.

Roy was adept with his Bushnell monocular and picked up the young ram right at the timberline, above camp about one and one-half miles away. "Maybe we should rest up and give it a shot tomorrow," he said, feeling his aching body.

"We can't hunt today anyhow, Roy," Bob said. "We'll get a fresh start at them tomorrow."

"That one's a bit young anyhow," noted Roy, putting away his monocular. He grinned. "Where there's one..."

The next morning, everyone was up at 5:30 A.M. The sheep hunters were anxious to get after them. They saw a sheep outfitter on the ride in and it is rumored that he was planning to hunt the same mountain. Roy never saw another sheep hunter, but with the limited range of a bighorn, it was wise to be up early. With the full-moon, the hunters didn't think they would find a ram in the open as many animals chose to feed, late. The Yellowstone fire had opened up some timber so glassing for them would be a little easier.

Bob led Roy up the ridge outside of camp to spot sheep on the mountain they had glassed before. When they scanned the high ground, all they saw were ewes and lambs. One young, sickle-horn ram appeared with the ewes, but was not the ram the pair sought. Roy had remembered a wildlife video concerning sheep hunting and had an idea.

"Bob, those sheep videos that I watched last month said that if the ewes and lambs were high on the mountain, the rams should be lower," guessed Roy his eyes glued to his hand-scope. "We need to look down in that burned timer."

With that, the couple shifted their glassing and began dissecting the timber. Bob broke up the slope into quadrants while Roy glassed up and down the slopes. Sheep hunting is usually a lot of looking, and the pair shifted between their hand-held optics and Bob's spotting-scope. Just when they wanted to glass more land, Bob found a legal ram.

"Look at this," whispered Bob. "I don't think we have to look any further. There's more rams with that one, down in the trees."

They crossed the small valley and climbed a finger of the burned timber, parallel to their quarry. Roy checked the wind and continued to stalk from a downwind position. Having climbed high enough, they stopped to check the sheep before moving forward. Checking his watch, Bob found the rams asleep in the timber at 10:00 A.M.

The pair exchanged the lead as they traversed the alternate draws and ridges toward the rams. They crossed the third draw and Roy thought they had one more ridge to go. They were running the rims of these ridges before they dropped off and became steep. Bob thought that their route through the last ravine would bring them within yards of the dozing rams.

Roy took one more look before the final stalk and cursed. The sheep had vanished. Actually, they had awakened and were trying to escape behind them about 80 yards downhill. Bob remained behind his binoculars while Roy dropped into a prone position with the Thompson rested on his fanny-pack. Bob tried to determine which ram was the best.

"Take the third ram back from the trees," commanded Bob, eyes still at his optics. "He looks to be the best one."

Roy saw one full-curl ram at 90 yards but then Bob stopped him before he could shoot.

"Hold it Roy, there's a better one below in the timber," he said excitedly.

"I see him, but I don't think I can thread the needle through those threes," said Roy. "Wait a minute, there he comes."

The trophy lined up with a hole through the trees. Roy aimed and then waited. A small ram stepped in front of his target and made Roy hold until the shot was clear. Once the young ram walked through, Roy sighted and squeezed off. The mountain exploded with scrambling bighorns while Roy's ram folded neatly.

"Do you think we got the biggest one, Bob?" Roy was still facing his fallen target.

"I don't know, but the ram you got is pretty damn good," said Bob.

The two watched the ram fall in a hole that would be some tricky climbing to get into.

"I'll head back for the packboard, Roy," said Bob. "You go dress 'em out."

When Bob left for the packboard, Roy glanced over to the fallen ram and dropped his video camera. The sheep had come back to life and was clawing uphill as if he hadn't been hit. Roy tore through the ravine to try a follow-up shot, thinking his ram prize was going to escape.

He ran down and slid when the dirt and rock gave way. He climbed back up and hoped that his ram would give him some kind of shot. Roy was blowing razor blades at 9700 feet on the ridge. The bighorn had not topped out yet on the next ridge. Gasping and coughing, Roy almost hoped he wouldn't have to shoot again and the ram would succumb to its wound.

Out of the timber ran the sheep, unimpaired, while Roy leveled his .309 JDJ for an offhand shot at 80 yards. Roy held his breath, sighted through his Burris 4x scope, and fired as the trophy ram fell, pole axed by a perfect shot through the spine. Bob joined Roy after catching up with the younger hunter.

"Boy, did we play dumb," gasped Bob, putting his big hand on Roy's shoulder. "Better make sure this time. Don't wanna run no more ridges on this hunt."

There wasn't anything to follow up with a spinal shot, but Roy made sure just the same. The 150 grain Hornaday had done its work behind 53 grains of IMR 4350. He found the first shot had clipped the top of the ram's shoulder blades, exiting the sheep with no fatal damage. It was 11:30 A.M. when Roy got the sheep.

Bob threw a steel tape around the horns and measured 36 inches. The bases were 15 inches in circumference with the horns carrying the mass all the way to the tips. He was broomed back a little and both men green-scored the ram at over 170 Boone & Crockett points. After the measurement and congratulations, Roy was enveloped by a feeling common of successful sheep-hunters.

Twenty-six years of waiting and hoping. But after months of planning and conditioning, the mental and equipment preparation was finally over. Roy didn't know if he would ever get to hunt bighorns again.

Many sheep hunters experience the same feelings after they get their ram. It was almost as if it would be better if they hadn't drawn a sheep tag. Roy's friends, acquaintances, and perhaps people that he never knew before, congratulate him over and over again. Everyone wished that they could have had the same experience. Roy faced the odds and won and that memory lived for him.

Roy Kern drew Wyoming bighorn sheep area number three in 1994, taking this trophy ram with his pistol. Roy was accompanied by long-time friend Bob Sexton, a retired game warden.

Chapter 6
A Little Help From My Friends

The trail glowed an eerie red through Sergeant Pat Clark's infrared rifle scope. It had just rained on this section of an enemy supply trail through South Vietnam. Pat's camouflage army poncho clung to him through the night. Mosquitos were thick and hungry, about as big as the bombers that were hammering the Viet Cong, miles away. Snipers like Sergeant Clark had been stationed along supply routes that constantly replenished Communist guerrillas in the country. The United States would give anything to stop the provisions to the Viet Cong in the south. Pat was one way to help achieve that objective.

Blood ran down Pat's forehead from a cut caused by a branch, mixed with insect repellant and was dropping into his left eye. His eye stung, but Pat dare not move now that the enemy was probably moving his way. Mosquitos were ignoring the ineffective repellant. The air strikes should send The Cong running right into Pat's ambush. He fought off fatigue caused by watching these trails for too long. Pat readjusted his M-14 sniper rifle, pointing it down the expected path of the enemy. It was 1964, just when the Vietnam War began to escalate in an attempt to stop the Viet Cong and protect South Vietnam's fledgling government. Exploding bombs in the distance kept interrupting the night's stillness.

Pat watched all night and into the morning until his squad leader relieved him at 9:00 A.M. Pat hooked up with another marksman named Harry. The two traveled through the foliage until they reached a point in the rear where a UH-1 helicopter could pick them up. They didn't follow a trail as they were wary of booby-traps set by both forces. Both of them had friends that had been wounded while attempting to advance on a trail. When they finally reached the landing-zone, they cautiously awaited the green huey that would take them to their fire base. They had been harassing the enemy for weeks in the bush. Other ambushes were more productive and produced better body counts. Pat had little time left in the country. He had orders directing him to Ft. Monmouth, New Jersey, about 50 miles south of New York City.

Clark was 18 years old and had plenty of time left in the service. Pat thought he was out of the woods when he left Vietnam. Troops at Ft.

Monmouth were assigned as a quick reaction force for problems in the Caribbean and Central-America. Pat wasn't in New Jersey very long before trouble erupted in the Dominican Republic.

Trouble had broken out and President Johnson ordered troops to the Dominican Republic to protect American citizens there and help keep the Communists from gaining power. Rebels had already captured parts of Santo Domingo.

Pat's 595th Combat Signal Company got the call late that morning in April, 1965. They were being mobilized for possible deployment to the Caribbean nation. Pat and his unit had worked hard all day when he was assigned to drive a deuce-and-a-half truck that night, down a highway to McGuire Air Force Base. The unit would depart for the Dominican Republic from there. It wasn't just the work that day that had made Pat tired. He had pulled duty the night before and patrolled Ft. Monmouth for security reasons. When the scattered convoy pulled onto the parkway, the tired buck sergeant clung to the truck's wheel.

The train rounded a turn when Pat's eyes couldn't stay open any longer. He fell asleep at the wheel. When he woke, the truck was leaving the road and was flipping down an embankment. Pat grimaced in pain from the weight of the truck door pinning down his back. The truck rolled again before slamming into a tree. Pat was knocked out. Luckily, military policemen were on the scene at once. They pulled Pat from the wreckage and called an ambulance from Ft. Monmouth.

After initial first aid, the dark-haired NCO was driven to St. Albin's Navy Hospital for treatment. Pat's military career came to an abrupt end that night on a dark highway in southern New York City. The Army discharged the paraplegic NCO and sent him to the Bronx Veteran's Administration Hospital near his home in Newark, New Jersey. Between the two institutions, Pat was hospitalized over one year. When he was released from the V.A., he wasn't going to let the accident stop him from the pursuit of his favorite pastimes: guns, hunting, and girls.

Although classified as a paraplegic, Pat could still hobble around on his metal crutches. He adapted to them quickly, but wasn't able to work. It was one year later when Pat met his future wife, Delores. The long-legged blonde married Pat later that year in New Jersey. He continued to chase after his other loves, too. The disabled veteran shuffled through the doors of Ledgewood Outdoorsman one day in search of a hunting rifle.

"How about this rifle, here," Pat pointed to a pretty 7mm lying beneath the glass at the store in his East Coast accent. "Can I put it up?"

Wally Needham, the owner of the store and a bear of a man, strode over and pulled the rifle out of the case. Pat hefted it, sighted down it's barrel and found it to his liking. Pat did his best to have Wally reduce the price of the gun but there was no budging the Scotchman.

"You're trying to screw me out of this rifle, Pat," raged Wally. "I can't give it away."

"I'm giving it my best shot," returned the stocky veteran, rocking on his new crutches. "I like the rifle, but at my terms."

The pair respected each other's ability to stand his ground for the contested rifle. It wasn't long before they joined each other for a pot of coffee and planned future hunts between them in the local area. They found a common love of hunting and were able to use that to begin a friendship. The disabled veteran obtained a permit which allowed him to shoot from a vehicle. He spent many hours on the stand looking for whitetail deer. They also engaged in groundhog shooting during the off season. Pat's real hunting didn't begin until he went west to Wyoming in 1972. Pat, his wife Dee, and their daughter, Christina moved to Story, Wyoming near Sheridan in the northeast corner of the state.

Pat and Dee settled into the small Wyoming town where he could escape the city pressures of the East Coast. Wally followed Pat to Wyoming two years later, but chose Cheyenne in the state's southeast corner to live. It wasn't until 1977 that the two planned a western hunt. Whitetail deer are best sought in Wyoming during Thanksgiving when they come into their rut. Pat had found the right property to hunt on from a vehicle. Wally drove to Story from Cheyenne where the pair wasted no time getting into good hunting country.

Conditions were ripe with six inches of new snow on the ground. A warm front invaded the region, casting fog into the valley. When Pat drove over hill utilizing the vehicle's hand controls, 50 whitetail stood before them in a large field. He quickly analyzed the situation with his keen eyesight.

"Not a buck in the bunch, Wally," said the combat veteran. "Wonder where they can be?"

"Let's just sit tight for awhile," said Needham, eyes at his binoculars. "With that many females to smell, a buck's gotta be close by."

Pat shut off the truck engine and reached for his optics to search for a buck as well. The fog was lifting and their glasses dissected the surrounding fields. Pat gripped his tighter, leaning forward.

"Got one," said Pat. "He's a five-point and pretty good too. Guess you won the toss for the first shot."

Wally dismounted the truck, found a rest to shoot from, and drilled the whitetail buck with his .270 Winchester at 200 yards. When they loaded the dressed animal, Wally witnessed the paraplegic's upper strength when he loaded the 145-lb. buck by himself.

In 1982, the pair booked a moose hunt in Canada with an outfitter who planned to hunt Pat from an all-terrain vehicle (ATV). Wally hunted with another guide. Pat's guide was ferrying him across a swampy area when the ATV got stuck in the middle of the bog. The guide left Pat with the ATV while he walked back to camp for tools to free the vehicle. Pat was left alone for hours, in sub-freezing temperatures. He was very cold and his feet concerned him as he has no feeling in them since his accident in 1964. He didn't know if his lower limbs were freezing. He couldn't walk out like the guide had done. His confidence was badly shaken and he became very upset when help finally arrived. Pat had undergone weeks in the bush in Vietnam but that was nothing compared to battling this handicap. This truly shook his self-confidence. Wally figured they should hunt in areas where Pat wouldn't have many difficulties arise. They needed a place where they could hunt from their vehicle.

Probably the animal Pat wanted to pursue most was an elk. They would have to find an area where they could kill an elk, practically from the truck's window. Needham's connections and information in his post at People's Sporting Goods in Cheyenne, revealed the perfect area in Northwest Wyoming.

Every year, the Wyoming Game & Fish Department does their best to reduce the bludgeoning elk populations of Yellowstone and Grand Teton National Parks. Although Yellowstone is closed to hunting, part of Grand Teton can be hunted by duly permitted hunters who are deputized by Park officials to thin the herds. Both herds pass through here on their way to the National Elk Refuge where they are fed supplemental feed during the winter. These hunts are governed by The Park Service and the weather. Natural predation on park elk was practically non-existent. Many environmentalists would like to see wolves reintroduced to help the problem. A lot of controversy has been aroused by this proposal, particularly among area ranchers. But in 1984 hunting was the only way to trim the herds through several areas north of Jackson Hole and a few in Montana. The areas were not difficult to access by road and offered hunters like Pat and Wally opportunities to harvest elk. When fall or winter snows became heavy, park elk started migrating to the National Elk Refuge. The trick was to be in the right place, at the right time and the hunt hinged on how good a marksman the hunter was. Needham arranged for a hotel room for four hunters to hunt the refuge during the second week of November, 1984.

Wally's teenaged, red headed son, Garry, culled a five-by-five bull on their first day after he drew a permit for hunting the refuge. The following day, Wally and Pat were allowed to drive into the refuge. They saw little in the course of the morning, glassing and driving around. When they stopped to eat lunch, Needham unpacked ham and cheese sandwiches they had prepared the night before. The sandwiches were barely unwrapped when Pat saw an elk herd coming across a ridge to their front.

"Let's just stay put, Wally," whispered the husky veteran. "They may come this way but if we move, for sure they're going elsewhere."

They must have parked on a natural elk route because it wasn't long until they were enveloped by wapiti. The main herd had advanced over the ridge, and broke into smaller groups that invaded the field. A small band turned toward them. Pat rolled down his window, poking his .300

Winchester from the truck's window. The herd was scampering through, about 70 yards distant when Wally found a fat spike bull bringing up the herd's rear.

"I got 'em dead in my sights," said Pat, steam still rising from his coffee mug on the truck's dashboard. "Spot the shots, Wally."

Two quick shots rang from Pat's window. The elk was hit. Pat sighted and led the bull for his third shot. The yearling elk was felled by the final shot, which broke the shoulder and clipped the heart. Wally dragged the spike over the foot-deep snow to the truck after he dressed it. He knew that there were always enough willing people around to help you load or drag a kill. Several hunters helped drag the bull into the truck. Wally harvested another elk on that same day, dropping a mature cow with one shot.

This was the place for a disabled person to hunt elk. Pat could either shoot from the vehicle or stagger a few yards to get a better field-of-fire.

Tony, a friend of Wally's, joined Wally and Pat the next year for the hunt. They chose to hunt the last week of October, 1985, in the same area. They arrived on a Friday in bitter, cold weather. The hunters had reserved a room at the same motel for their week-long adventure. Pat drove to the same spot where he had shot the spike the preceding year. Tony and Wally drove to a point where they could watch long distances. Wally focused his optics on a dark spot, about three miles away. Soon, both hunters were watching the same spot. As it came closer, they were disappointed when they recognized the object as a mounted park ranger. When the ranger spotted their truck, he turned his horse to meet them. About the time he rode up to their Ford, Wally found another dark spot coming from the same region the ranger had come from.

"You fellas ought to wear orange out here so we won't confuse you with elk," kidded Wally. "Is that your buddy coming from where you just came?"

"I was the only one back there," said the ranger turning to depart. "You better take another look."

Just then, the three discerned the spot as three large bull elk, coming their way. The bulls were three miles away so the pair stepped from the truck and advanced 100 yards. The elk kept coming their way as if drawn by a magnet. For 10 minutes, the two hunters drooled as the bulls came straight at them. When they had moved to within 200 yards, Tony opened up with his Remington pump .30-06. Due to the heavy, round-nosed bullets and the rifle's zero, Tony couldn't connect initially with the largest bull. Eventually, he put two rounds through the elk's shoulder and heart.

The next morning, Tony accompanied Pat for good luck. The two hunters parked their Ford in a likely spot on the elk refuge. When daybreak came at last, Pat was going crazy at the sight of so many elk. An elk herd weaved their way, trying to escape past Pat's truck.

"Take the bull on the left," said Tony, glued to his binoculars. "He looks like a royal bull."

The ex-sniper sighted through his powerful rifle-scope, pulled the trigger, and watched the magnificent animal go down. Each of them knew that when elk are in their migration mode, they have a lot of adrenaline in their system and can be resilient. Even though the first shot knocked the bull off his feet, Pat had to fire several more shots before the animal succumbed. Pompous park officials who were at the scene made Pat walk to the animal as it may have needed a coup-de-grace shot. Pat hobbled across a ditch, fell and yelled for help.

"Wally!"

Help arrived to pull Pat from the greasy channel. Wally couldn't help laughing at the sight of Pat wallowing in the mud.

"Damn, you look like a walrus in that hole," he chuckled.

"Cut it out, dumb-ass," wailed Pat, in his New Jersey accent. "Get me outta here."

When they arrived at the fallen bull, they couldn't help but be impressed with the creature's black features and mass. They thought, it was a shame that the elk didn't have more symmetrical antlers, as it might have been a candidate for the record books.

Pat Clark had the best record for getting elk among his hunting party that visits Jackson nearly every year. He was nine-for-nine on elk up there because he was blessed with excellent eyesight, could shoot very well and always seemed to be where the elk migrate. Whether luck or knowledge of animal habits, it produced elk for Pat.

Several times, Pat hit elk only to see them downed by another hunter. These elk were terminally hit by Pat, but the rules governing elk hunts in the park awarded the elk to the hunter who dropped the animal. Elk can carry a lot of lead before they die.

Pat had found the perfect area to hunt elk in with his disability. Pat's friends were instrumental in helping him hunt effectively. They didn't treat him like someone who's handicapped—they actually expected more from him. He learned that he hunted best with a little help from his friends.

Pat Clark with a dandy Wyoming white deer he took from his truck. Wyoming allows mobility disabled people to hunt from their vehicle.

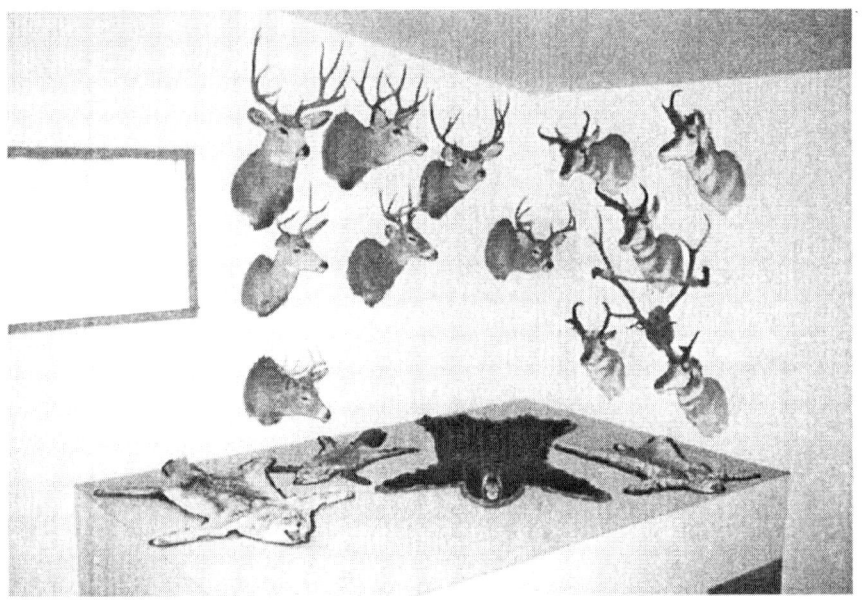

Just a few of Pat's trophy game mounts he has collected over the years.

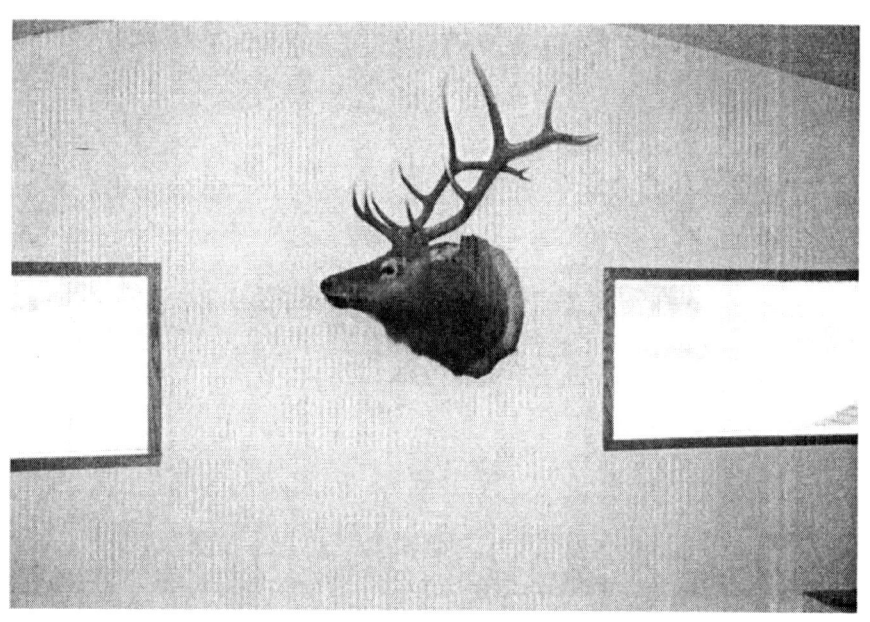

Pat's trophy, seven-by-six bull elk he harvested on a late-season migration hunt near Jackson, Wyoming. Pat uses his Army sniper skills to execute long shots on elk in that area.

Chapter 7
Two Wheel Drive

It was the spring of 1973 when the stout 20 year old Jerry Johnson hopped into his pickup truck, thoughts of getting a coyote like the one he watched voraciously feed on a fresh-killed cow was on his mind. He didn't know what had killed the cow, but he knew that the calves would be born soon and any predator was unwelcome on his father's farm especially at that time. He was concerned about the dog that he had seen through his binoculars about one mile away. Ranchers didn't like coyotes and he had caught one red-handed. He didn't know that his short truck ride would change the rest of his life.

He gained speed, oblivious to the twisting dirt road beneath him. His window was down, allowing the west Nebraska wind to fly through his brown hair. While Jerry stepped on the pedal, he had thoughts of race car drivers on his mind. The truck speedometer was showing 70 mph. When he hit the banked part of the road, he slowed slightly and his mind was absorbed with the bandit coyote rather than his dangerous stunt. Suddenly, the truck's left wheels began to lift. Jerry over-corrected and his body hurdled through a harrowing rollover. Jerry was thrown from the vehicle and hit a rock with his back. He tried to stand but his legs wouldn't respond to his brain.

Jerry was scared and lay still rather than possibly hurt himself more. Two hours went by before he heard another vehicle. Jerry's father, Dewey, arrived at the scene and rushed to assist his son, hurrying him to the local hospital in North Platte, Nebraska. Jerry was quickly transferred to St. Luke's Hospital in Denver, Colorado and was put under the care of Dr. Stephen Samuelson, a neurologist. His prognosis for Jerry wasn't good. Jerry had suffered spinal cord damage and would probably never walk again.

Jerry's railroad career was wiped out along with what he thought would be any hunting that he would do in the future. Jerry had just began working for Union Pacific and was liking his job. Jerry loved to hunt! It was his most serious hobby and pursuit. How would he be able to continue a hobby that requires much physical prowess? Jerry spent about one month at St. Luke's and then was transferred to Swedish Medical Center in the same city and eventually arrived at Craig Hospital for rehabilitation.

"If I can't do what I want to do, I'd rather be dead," adamantly said Jerry. "I wasn't gonna let no little accident stop me from hunting again."

Jerry was intent on regaining his strength. He pushed himself to resume his normal life on the ranch. He got back onto the tractor with the help of a hydraulic lift that he and his father constructed. He drove with the aid of hand controls for his Ford Truck. The state of Nebraska issued him a permit that allowed him to shoot from a vehicle. Authorized by this piece of paper, Jerry was hunting deer and antelope again that fall of 1978.

A four-wheel all terrain vehicle was an asset for him when it comes to upland bird hunting. North Platte, Nebraska was blessed with a good pheasant population. Sometimes, Jerry ranged his father's farm in his ATV. He was as conscious of creating good bird habitat as if they were his corn fields. In this manner, he was able to keep about 100 pheasants on the place. Thousands of Canada geese spent winter along the Platte River with the bountiful grain fields nearby. Jerry has a chocolate Labrador retriever who often joined him on the bird hunt. When colder weather sets in, he retreated to a couple of goose pits that he has constructed on the farm. Goose hunting from a pit was tailor-made for someone with a mobility impairment. Years spent hunting them has made Jerry a very competent water fowler. He also had access to a farm that many Merrium's turkey called home.

He no longer chased turkey in orthodox fashion, donning camouflage and squeaking a gobbler call. He drove a lot for turkey and was fortunate to have entry to a farm where they weren't hunted by the general public. Jerry was successful and put many wild birds in the roaster. It didn't matter to Jerry what he hunted, just that he enjoyed the hunt.

Most able bodied hunters would be well satisfied with the type of success that Jerry had hunting game. He rarely ate meat from the store and subsisted mainly on the larder from his hunting escapades. Although he had shot four-by-four mule deer before, he usually was satisfied with smaller bucks which added to his freezer of game meat. Elk are also on his hunting list. Succulent cows are his choice for filling the freezer. Bulls were harder to get and usually didn't satisfy his taste buds like the more palatable females. He usually chased after antelope each year in his pickup truck. Most of the time, he will lay an ambush at a natural crossing point or waterhole though his four-by-four was important equipment on these hunts.

In 1988, Jerry had the opportunity to hunt prime ranchland for elk with an organization in Colorado. Jerry suffered a minor heart attack that year and was once again committed to Denver hospitals. When he was out of bed again, he went through Craig Hospital where he met recreation director, Sam Andrews. Sam introduced Johnson to Sid Sellers, head of the Denver based hunting group, Outdoor Buddies. Outdoor Buddies worked with mainly mobility-disabled people and had access to prime hunting territory throughout the state. Sellers arranged a hunt for Jerry on a local ranch that received minimal hunting pressure. The group was successful in helping disabled hunters from all over the country.

Jerry was coupled with another paraplegic, Glen, from Arkansas.

The two were driven over to the ranch shop where they were greeted by the ranch foreman, with two large cups of coffee. They talked about what type of elk they might see on their forthcoming hunt. The disabled pair were assured that the elk on this particular ranch weren't easlily spooked due to the low hunting pressure. Finding a large bull might be a problem, but there were plenty of cows to choose from. Both men carried licenses that empowered them to shoot either sex of wapiti on the ranch or in the entire area. Glen had never hunted them, so he wasn't selective. He just wanted some elk for the dinner table as he had heard that they were delicious.

Jerry wasn't going to be particular either, though he drew the straw for first shot if the situation arose. Jerry was loaded into a truck cab while Glen was hoisted into the rear bed with his wheelchair. He was given a support for a prospective shot.

The foreman scoured a couple of fields and two canyons looking for game the two hunters could fix their sights on. They located elk in the first valley, but couldn't get close to the herd. When the foreman looked over to Jerry, he winked and said "Don't give up on me yet, Jerry. There's plenty of places to find elk on this ranch."

He drove to a nearby ridge where a small elk herd appeared in the timber about halfway up. Perfect. This was the opportunity they were searching for. Having the first shot, Jerry quickly aimed his .30-60 at the bull, a six-point shepherding his dozen cows through the timber with increasing speed. He was a large, symmetrical six-by-six with ivory antler-tines; a good trophy for any hunter.

At 80 yards, Jerry could pick his shot on the huge bull. He knew it was wise to aim for the biggest, most lethal target on the animal: the lungs. After he shot, Jerry instantly knew the animal was dead and inside a dozen steps, he was.

Glen quickly pointed his rifle at one of the larger cows in the bull's harem. He was being coached into the shot by one of the hunt organizers. Glen dropped the cow with a single shot from his rifle as well. After much congratulatory ceremoney, the elk were loaded into their truck for the group to haul to a local game processor.

Jerry took his bull straight to a taxidermist in Denver. With a bull like this, a trophy mount was a fitting crown to a memorable hunt. Outdoor Buddies estimated the ivory-tined beast at well over 300 Boone & Crockett points, a respectabel bull elk for any hunter. Jerry returned to hunt with Colorado's disabled hunting group for elk almost every year after that first hunt. He rarely went away empty-handed, though not with bulls that rated as high as that first elk. Actually, most of his elk were cows due to ranch requirements and Jerry's preference for the tasty meat. One trophy bull was enough for him.

The paraplegic had good success along the Niobrara River in Nebraska for mule deer. Gaining access to excellent hunting hadn't been a real problem for Jerry. He had access to several ranches along the river where he could hunt easily from the automobile. He usually took along a friend for back-up but that wasn't always the case. He took a fine buck in 1989 by himself near the Niobrara.

Jerry had spent most of the day looking for bucks on the ranch. He could find them but none were in good range. After struggling along the river all morning, he steered his black Ford to a nearby canyon after lunch. He took a snooze, knowing that mule deer weren't active at midday. After his nap, Jerry snaked into the ravine with his truck, slowly and watched for any movement in every direction. He spied some erect ears poking out of the buck brush to his left.

He halted his slow-moving vehicle until he could focus his binoculars on his subject. It was usually the ears or white butt that gave a mule deer away. Jerry sighted a 20 inch four-point that was staring right at him at 200 yards. Any closer and the deer would have bounced away in the fashion mule deer are known for. Jerry's time was precious. He lined up his .30-06 from the truck window. Holding his breath he squeezed the trigger and broke the deer's neck with a perfect shot. There was no need to follow up that round. Maneuvering his truck through the brush to access the fallen buck was more difficult. He dressed, quartered, and loaded the venison with no assistance. "If you can't get a deer on the river," Jerry would say, "It's your own fault."

Given his limitations, any deer was a trophy and any tag not filled by him was not really his fault.

Jerry thought back to another elk hunt on Oak Creek near Steamboat Springs, Colorado in October, 1989. Once again, Outdoor Buddies' president, Sid Sellers, had obtained permission for a band of handicapped sportsmen to hunt on a prime ranch. Four mobility-disabled elk hunters joined with Jerry to make the hunt.

It was a dry fall with no snow to drive the elk from the security of their timber jungle. Despite the weather, Sid and company staged a fantastic experience for the impaired hunters. The first lucky hunter went home with meat from a cow elk on the second day. Everyone else felt like they were barking up a tree with the weather so warm. Jerry was seeing elk, but they were at distances that he was uncomfortable shooting from. Sid made a long hunt out of the affair due to the unseasonable temperatures.

When Jerry saw one of those elk at long distance, he decided to give it a shot. He had time to set up on a fallen tree and focused his rifle-scope on a cow 400 yards, across the park. He pulled the trigger and then heard the sound of a bullet striking flesh. He had executed a lung-shot that brought the elk down within 20 yards. One Jerry has been able to take down an elk despite his disadvantage.

During September of 1991, Jerry drew an antelope permit for an area near Ault, Colorado, east of Ft. Collins. He paired up with another handicapped gunner, Tom Martin, to hunt the ranch that he had acquired permission on for three days. Both hunters found that they couldn't compete with normal hunters that were on the ranch concurrently. The pair would have been able to fill out the first day, but because of their disadvantaged position other "well" hunters continually beat them to an antelope sighted. After a frustratingly busy weekend, most of the "healthy" hunters went home on Sunday night. Jerry was able to score on a medium sized buck that Monday after everyone had left.

Jerry was driving around a draw when he spotted an antelope moving his way. He immediately stopped the truck and waited for the animal to get closer. When the goat stopped at the sight of the strange vehicle, obscured by brush, Jerry lined up his Heckler & Koch .30-06 on him at 150 yards. One running shot was all that Jerry needed to bring the buck down. Loading the animal wasn't much of a problem due to Jerry's upper body strength and experience with a wheelchair.

He had the opportunity to hunt Oak Creek again in 1991. Roger Brandl was hunting with Jerry again that year but without the help of Outdoor Buddies. There was 12 inches of snow on the ranch with more coming down. It was a hair-raising drive to Steamboat from North Platte. They made it and negotiated the snow with their ATV. They stayed at the ranch so there was no problem with cold nights in a tent. On the second day, the two wheeled into a drainage that was crisscrossed with fresh elk tracks. Once they saw what potential the valley had, they moved very little, not wanting to scare the game out.

While glassing from a snowy bank, three elk pushed their noses out of the trees across a stream. It was under 400 yards and gave Jerry the confidence to try a shot as he remembered the preceding year. Roger positioned Jerry so he was solidly supported. Roger backed off when Jerry gave him the sign that he would shoot. One 180 grain bullet from his .30-06 broke the shoulder on a fat cow elk. She went straight down. Roger paced off the distance at 350 yards from Jerry and his rifle. They collected the cow and continued hunting for Brandl's elk. Roger wanted to tag a bull with his permit.

The next day, the team snaked their way up a mountain checkered with numerous elk tracks. They had to four-wheel their way up the steep hillside, but once they ascended to the top, their reward was an elk paradise. One hundred elk came out of the timber atop the mount. They maneuvered the ATV for a better shot, then Roger struck out on foot. Jerry stayed with the ATV, as the motor made too much noise. Fifteen minutes, half an hour, 45 minutes and then a single volley broke the stillness of the mountaintiop.

When Roger came back for Jerry and their machine, his hands were bloody and were proof to Jerry that the shot had been successful. Roger had killed a five-by-five bull as other elk stood paralyzed in the trees. The commotion forced out a seven-point, or royal bull, that would have been and easy shot. Roger had his bull lying, though, so the royal escaped.

In 1992, Jerry undertook a horseback hunt for elk near Craig, Colorado with his partner, Roger Brandl.

Jerry even participated on a horseback elk hunt near Craig, Colorado. Outfitter, Jerry Woolsey, advertises for disabled clients, taking on Jerry and his partner, Roger that year. One would think that horseback-hunting would be difficult for someone who has no use of his legs due to the leg work involved. Jerry was an accomplished horseman but he found that having legs is important when riding uneven ground.

Roger and Jerry drove to Craig in October. They stayed one night in Craig and Woolsey. When they started out the next morning. Jerry didn't figure on a ten-mile ride to gain access to Woolsey's hunting area. On their way in, another disabled hunter gave them a scare while he was on his ride out from the previous hunt. The quadripligec sent shivers through the entire party when he performed a somersault over his horse's head when the mount bucked. Having no use of his limbs, this individual had to be led down the trail. No one was sure what made this horse think he was in a rodeo, but fortunately the quadriplegic landed in the trail's dust, unhurt. At least Jerry had use of his arms to help guide the horse. This guy's landing stunned him.

They proceeded down the trail. Jerry shifted his weight around in the saddle to stay balanced on his horse, the earlier accident fresh in his mind. About three quarters of the way down the path, they had to cross a wide stream. Jerry rode into the water nervously. When his steed suddenly decided to jump the last steam, Jerry went over the horse's neck and into a mudhole along the creek. Members of the hunting party dismounted and tried hoisting him back into the saddle. But the mount was jumpy and the rider unsettled, so the party wrestled for 30 minutes to get mud-covered Jerry back aboard.

Jerry thought that booking such a hunt with his condition, was maybe a bad idea. The ride left him tired and unsettled. He couldn't stop thinking about the other man's fall, his own and about how much worse it could be been for them both. When they arrived at the base camp, Jerry needed two days to recompose himself in camp while Roger hunted the ridges and basins rearby.

On the morning of their second day, Roger scored on a raghorn bull he found feeding on a ridge a few miles from camp. Jerry felt the need to pull himslef together after seeing Roger's bull and hearing his story.

Maybe I can score after all, he thought. There's no reason to quit hunting before I've even started just because of a little spill.

Jerry got back on his horse the third morning. They would scour the timber above camp for some elk Roger had seen the previous day. When Jerry maneuvered his horse into the trees, he could smell strong dank, elk musk. He was helped off the mount and spent all morning watching a highly used game trail. He sat all morning and at 10:00 A.M., he heard crashing on the trail. Jerry froze, eyes fixed on the opening ahead, rifle at the ready. The paraplegic could shoot either sex on his game permit, but he thought after paying for a guided hunt, he wanted another good bull to bring home. His eyes peered into the dark jungle and extracted a group of cow elk heading his way. Jerry's eyes frantically wanted to grow horns on the female's heads.

On his fourth day, Jerry again took a stand in the timber, hoping to waylay a bull elk. He remained absolutely still during his ambush near an opening in the forest. When he started to move, a large spike bull pushed out of the trees and danced into the clearing. Once again, Jerry had his rifle up, tracking the youngster while still hoping there was a bigger bull. The spike turned, posed and made for a tempting shot. Jerry fought back the urge to drop the young bull though anticipating a larger elk. Jerry continued to wait along the trail. He was feeling drowsy after having been up since early hours that morning. When he was nodding off, a crunching sound from behind alerted him. He turned to see a bull crashing through the trees, its nostrils full of the dreaded man-scent at close range.

It was no use, Jerry knew that you don't usually pursue an elk that has been spooked and he couldn't follow the elk anyway. When his guide picked him up late that morning, Jerry felt he had experienced plenty of adventure for one day, his last in the wilderness elk region. He loaded up and rode for camp where the crew was preparing for the journey out. It may have been time to leave but Jerry wasn't finished yet. He still had an elk tag to fill. Riding through some trees and part way through their trip out, Jerry smelled the dank elk scent that almost every elk hunter has sniffed before. He quickly unloaded from his horse so he could take a shot.

He caught glimpses of a six-by-six bull shuffling behind a curtain of dense timber. Jerry tried to maneuver for the shot, dragging himself back and forth to catch sight of the heavy bull elk. It was like finding an apparition that was floating through the trees. Finally, Jerry saw the bull half-hidden by the brush. He aimed his rifle, caught a sight picture and then fired. Wood flew from a withered pine tree, Jerry had missed his mark. The bull faded into the foliage with a clatter of broken tree limbs, never to be seen again. Jerry could get no second shot.

They continued the ride out until the horses began to spook, Jerry worried about getting dumped and hurt on his way home from a hunt he probably shouldn't have undertaken. He saw what was causing the stock to be unsettled when he glimpsed a black bear scrambling back into his tangled domain. It was hard to figure who was frightened worse by the encounter. Even if Jerry had a chance at the bruin, he carried no license that would afford him the right to hunt a bear. What they wanted to see were more elk so Jerry could get another crack at a 13th-hour wapiti. At this point, Jerry wasn't choosey about clobbering a big bull. They did see more elk, but they were safe on private ground where they couldn't shoot. It was a hair raising experience, but Jerry had to undertake it, otherwise he may have never known what his limitations were.

Jerry had been through it all. Tough outdoor experiences had both recharged his confidence and shown him where he must not go. He didn't let his predicament stop him from the sport that he enjoyed the most, hunting. He continually looked for ways to help other handicapped enjoy hunting. Jerry eventually became head of the Nebraska chapter of Outdoor Buddies.

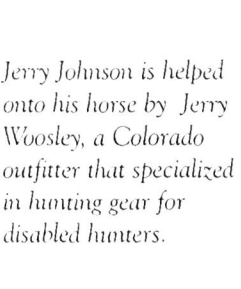
Jerry Johnson is helped onto his horse by Jerry Woosley, a Colorado outfitter that specialized in hunting gear for disabled hunters.

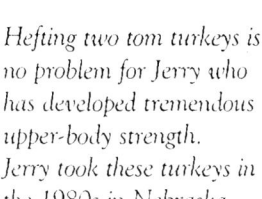
Hefting two tom turkeys is no problem for Jerry who has developed tremendous upper-body strength. Jerry took these turkeys in the 1980s in Nebraska.

Jerry, right, participates in an "Outdoor Buddies" ice-fishing trip in Nebraska.

Goose-hunting usually doesn't involve much movement. Jerry participates in the sport in his native, Nebraska.

Chapter 8
Close to My Heart

Ken Hall of Laramie, Wyoming had undergone two major heart operations, with eight coronary bypasses. The heart operations slowed him down and caused serious doubts in his abilities, but Ken refused to let heart difficulties stop him from the sport he enjoyed the most. Because of these heart operations, he was forced to undergo intensive rehabilitation. But Ken thought that hunting seriously again was the best rehabilitation that he could do.

Ken went on to hunt bighorn sheep in his native Wyoming, one year after his first operation. The following year, he took down a fine six-point bull elk near his hometown. He guided his heart surgeon to successive antelope bucks near Laramie in the mid-1980s and continued to enjoy shooting sports. Ken worked for outfitters and guided for elk and antelope. He recovered form his heart problems fully and thanked hunting for his strong recovery.

His first heart difficulty happened during January of 1982 while he was working in Wichita, Kansas on hail-damaged mobile homes. Ken was looking forward to working for an Afton, Wyoming outfitter, Billy Petersen. He would be working as a guide for hunters looking for elk in Wyoming's massive Grey's River region. Billy was planning to have Ken work in one of his lower Grey's River camps. The day after having an enormous supper, Ken started having stomach-problems. He drove to Wesley Medical Center, where he suffered a heart attack. The attack was mild and as he stabilized, doctors talked him into surgery, based on the tests performed on him. His first thought was to call his wife, Toni, who had stayed in Laramie while Ken was fixing trailers.

"Toni, I'm really scared!" Ken admitted. I don't know if I'll be able to guide this fall. I'll be lucky to do anything."

Dr. James P. Byrne told Ken that mental attitude has ninety percent of a successful operation. A good demeanor make's all the difference in the world. Wesley Medical Center had diagnosed Ken as having a totally blocked, right coronary artery. Heart bypass surgery would be the operation that would save Ken. While he waited for his operation on January 20th, he undertook an exercise program in walking around the hospital.

Every day he stretched out and increased his distance with every walk. He bought a pair of White Packers riding and walking boots and used them for every walk. Ken also bought a twenty-gauge shotgun for hunting back in Laramie. He was going to survive this operation. The thoughts of the two pieces of equipment kept his mind focused on the future and kept him from thinking about the serious operation he was to undergo.

Ken was up to walking two miles everyday before his operation. Toni was always at his side, urging him on.

Dr. Byrne operated on his new patient for four hours and constructed three bypasses in the damaged organ. When Ken awoke after surgery, Toni was right by his side. Their determination would not let him fall as he sped toward recovery. Ken's operation was on a Wednesday and by Saturday, he was busy breaking in those White Packers for fall hunting. By Sunday, he was walking almost one mile. Toni flew back home days after the surgery while Ken stayed with his sister in Wichita until he was well enough for the 7000 feet elevation of Laramie. High altitude is always harder to breathe in recovery from a heart operation.

By February 2nd, Ken was able to fly home and there he continued to walk every day. It was paramount that he stay away from stress, arguments and heavy labor for a period of time. He had to reduce anything that would make his heart work harder. Before his release from Wesley, he and Dr. Byrne had many opportunities to talk about hunting, which wet the Doctor's curiosity. Byrne told that if he could walk five miles then he could ride horseback again. Ken continued walking further and further with insatiable determination. By summer, he was riding his horse when and soon got a call from an outfitter requesting help.

Bob Lowe, owner of Arrowhead Outfitters, called Ken during early summer of 1982 wanting Ken to cook for him on bighorn sheep hunts that fall. Sheep hunting was usually a high altitude affair so Ken wanted Bob to know that he may not be able to handle it. Bob decided to test him on a preseason scouting trip into the Bridger-Teton Wilderness. Bob usually took at least one week to scout for sheep before his clients arrive. That way, they spend time looking at sheep and not for them.

Lowe didn't have a grasp on what Ken's limitations were. The two argued over Ken's wages and Bob demanded physical camp chores, although they agreed to be cautious about the elevation factor. When the pair became comfortable about the working arrangement, Ken stayed on to cook while Bob and his hunters looked for sheep. Fat brook trout supplemented Ken's diet, as the outdoorsman pulled many from nearby creeks during the day. Since Ken was there to cook, Bob would only let him pursue elk during the day when the season arrived. Elk were usually timber-hugging creatures during daylight hours.

When Ken found an elk herd, they had to retreat to a steep slope even though he found walking difficult. Elk hunting at midday is a hard job. He hunted the slope one day and the rough walking sent sharp pains through his chest. His heart started racing and he reached for his bottle of nitroglycerin. In a few moments, all of his methodical therapy, planning, and hopes seemed gone on that timbered slope. Ken thought very hard about dying so many miles from his loved ones. It scared him to die in a remote wilderness when he wasn't even hunting effectively.

Enough was enough. Ken decided that an elk was too hard for him to hunt. He continued cooking for Arrowhead Outfitters through four successful bighorn sheep hunts. He learned much about recovery from heart surgery with the help of Wyoming's pristine wilderness.

When he returned home to Laramie, Ken decided to hunt only antelope as they are less demanding than other game. Ken hunted an area north of town where he knew a willing rancher. Ken ventured onto the ranch alone for he had built his confidence during sheep camp. Toni knew where he was hunting, as did the landowner. Ken played around with those antelope all day. Since antelope were plentiful on the RO-ranch, Ken could be choosy about the buck he wanted. He hunted, mainly from the truck, because he didn't want to get far from his citizen's band radio. It had been about one month since his heart racing episode near the sheep camp, a feeling he definitely wanted to avoid. Spying four bucks far from his vehicle, Ken planned a strategy that would take him closer. Antelope in this area seemed to like crossing the road at a certain point. Perhaps they crossed because they were funnelled that way by the fences. Maneuvering his truck closer, Ken found a ditch that he could hide the truck in. He didn't have to venture too far before he found a spot that gave him good observation and fields-of-fire. Now, all he had to do was wait. After all he had been through, a little waiting was nothing. Four bucks appeared like dots along the fence line extending from Ken. The biggest buck had ivory-tipped horns over 14 inches high and a good mass.

Ken decided that he couldn't be too selective or his wife would worry about him. A 14-inch horned antelope was pretty good after surviving a heart attack. In they marched, intent on pastures or water-holes on the other side of the road.

May as well let them come in as far as they will, thought Ken. No need to drag an animal any further than need be.

When they were within 70 yards, Ken cut loose with his 6mm Remington and down went one fine antelope buck. A combination of patience and experience spelled success for Ken that October. He wasn't going to let a heart problem stop him from what he enjoyed most.

The twenty-gauge shotgun Ken had purchased in Wichita was put to good use that fall in pursuit of waterfowl. Ken had permission from several Laramie area ranches to jump-shoot teal and mallards off ranch irrigation ditches. Several mornings, Ken jumped many mallards off of the ditches. He would sneak in as close as he could when he spotted ducks, then rush in to spook the birds. Before the birds flew out of range, he would score.

Ken still wanted to hunt larger game, but elk and deer were too taxing for Ken to try that year. He thought about those elk up in the wilderness that made his heart race. Elk could make any man's heart jump, but not like Ken's that day. With one season behind him after undergoing major heart surgery, Ken thought about applying for a bighorn sheep permit in 1983. It must have been all those days in sheep camp that previous year that made Ken apply for one of the most strenuous of hunts. When he opened that letter from the Wyoming Game & Fish that summer, it was like a dream come true. All those years of hoping, applying, and dreaming had finally paid off. Now he really had a reason to get in shape. Ken had many doubts about his ability when he thought about those days at the sheep camp, but he knew Bob would help him get his much desired ram.

Ken redoubled his rehabilitation program and increased the number of miles he walked hoping that it would help him reap a trophy sheep that fall. Ken built up his strenth by walking and riding all summer and set a target date in mid-October. Bighorns would migrate into the Whiskey Mountain area of his hunting region as fall progressed into winter. Bob always liked to hunt the territory late in the hunting season for this reason. Ken didn't object because the more time before the hunt commenced, the more rehabilitation he could do.

It was mid-October before he felt he was ready. Ken undertook the 300 mile drive to Riverton, Wyoming where Bob lived at the time. When he pulled into Bob's driveway, the stocky outfitter had everything ready for the hunt. They both rode in Bob's truck, pulling a trailer with two horses for the adventure. Whiskey Mountain is within 100 miles from Riverton and upon arrival they erected a small base camp at its foot.

The pair wondered which way would be the best approach to the mountain.

"I don't want to get in that rough country on the side of that one mountain but that's probably where the rams will be," Bob said while grilling streaks for supper.

"Mabye we can find rams moving into that country," Ken replied.

With that, the two retired to the small tents Bob had brought for the hunt. It wouldn't be that far-fetched to say that Ken counted sheep to help him sleep that night. The next morning after a quick breakfast Bob saddled horses and off they went. Bod was hoping to find a ram that wouldn't be too difficult for Kent to stalk. They rode some flat country on top of the mountain, always looking off into the breaks below. There seemed to be plenty of female sheep and lambs already on the winter range, but none of the rams they sought. Ken insisted that Bob build him a fire that first day. He was getting chilled, but mostly suffered from lack of self-confidence.

The first day ended with observation of some juvenile rams, but still, nothing legal. Wyoming required at legal bighorn sheep to be at least three-quarter curl, but Ken would take the first legal ram that he saw. His .257 Roberts was the chosen rifle for the hunt. He had years of confidence invested in it. Ken hand-loads his own ammunition so the cartridges were loaded to maximum velocity and accuracy. He had wanted to bring his own horse for the hunt, but Bob's stock were more reliable.

The pair chose to hunt areas of the mountain yet untravelled by them. Once again, they sighted lots of ewes and lambs on the second day but not even a young ram. The strategy was akin to their first day with a lot of glassing. When they came back into camp, Bob suggested they would try a different part of the mountain the next day.

"I'd like to try the west side of the mountain, Ken," said Bob. "We'll get into a little rougher country but that's where the big ones gotta be. Rams and ewes only come together during early December for the rut. They might start thinking about doing that now." I've heard that rams like the tough country," said Ken, shivering in his blanket from the cold night. "I think it's that way with any wild, male animal."

Bob cooked hot cereal for breakfast the next day, saddled horses and led them to the desired area. Bob didn't want to ride in too rough a country; he didn't know how much his big friend could take. They saw some ewes and lambs like yesterday but this time when they stopped to glass a ridge, they finally saw some rams.

They maneuvered the horses closer and then tied them up. Like all sheep guides, Bob knew that the best way to finish up the hunt was on foot. They lost sight of the sheep while they snaked through the timber hillside between them and the rams. As the trees petered out, they became more alert. Bob and Ken relied mostly on their eyes for locating their game, but sometimes they heard the sheep too. Rocks started rolling as bighorn rams were making their escape behind them.

"Quick, Ken!" exclaimed Bob. "Get to where you can shoot."

Ken scrambled over some rock towards a knoll where he had a solid bench-rest. Bob was observing and waited for the sheep to come into the open. When they arrived, Bob didn't have to coach Ken as to which ram was legal. Ken had done his homework and judged the horn size for himself. The first ram walked around a rock point but wasn't legal. Hall looked hard through his three by nine riflescope and wanted to imagine a few more inches of horn onto the immature ram. When the second ram appeared, Ken had no doubt as to its legality. The bighorn was easily a few inches beyond the three-quarter minimum. It was a waiting game now as he watched the sheep march closer. Ken thought he could make a 400 yard but as long as they were coming, he held out. It wasn't long until the string of rams were within 300 yards. Ken still had his eyes riveted on the second ram.

Snuggling closer to his .257 Roberts, Ken touched off a shot that hit the ram in the shoulder. He chambered another round to hit the sheep in the same spot. The ram started to turn away as Ken aimed the third shot, but the bullet hit the ram's horn and knoched him down. The fourth shot anchored the bighorn in the neck and broke it.

"Great shooting," Bob praised as he looked through his binoculars. "I think that your first shot would have done him in, though. Didn't you see the bigger ram in that band?"

Ken didn't care. He had just survived major heart surgery 21 months prior and now he claimed one of North America's greatest trophies, the bighorn sheep. When they reached the ram, Bob threw his steel measuring tape around the horns and recoreded 32 inches in length with 15 inch bases of circumference. Ken relished eating barbecued sheep-ribs like he had read about in his journals. Ken has accomplished one year of serious hunting since his operation in Wichita. Ken had made it all the way back, but he still was cautious of his heart.

The following year, Ken hunted closer to home, only 40 miles away. Ranchers in the Arlington, Wyoming sector had been complaining about elk harassing their alfalfa fields and stacked hay. The Wyoming Game & Fish administered a depredation hunt in the affected zone in the early 1980s, but with little success. Wyoming continued to have hunting seasons for elk along Rock Creek which receives drainage from the north slope of nearby Snowy Range. The fertile soil and abundant water make for easy alfalfa growth. Elk were adaptable creatures, so when they moved out of their natural mountain enviornment, they conformed to the swampy Rock Creek drainage north of Interstate 80. Most elk hunters wear cleated mountain boots for their hunting. Along Rock Creek, hipwaders were more suitable footwear in the boggy terrain.

Ken met a hunting buddy with similar heart problems for the excursion. Smitty accompanied Ken to the district the day before the season started. They scouted the creek and found several possibilities, including one monstrous six-point bull. Elk season for Snowy Range didn't begin until October 15th and deer season began today, the 1st so most hunters were hunting deer. But Ken and Smitty had patterned the elk in order to find out where they fed and the swampy holes they slept in. The trick was to catch them between the two sectors since elk seldom feed during daylight. When the two embarked into the district the next day, Ken could hear a bull tearing up a tree somewhere in the quagmire. They tried to reach the animal, but scuba gear would have been required. This bull had found a safe haven from the hunters.

They seperated, with Ken working his way around the marsh until he sensed something seemingly pulling at his shoulder. Turning ever so slightly, he saw another nice six-point bull herding cows into a opening. At 200 yards, the monarch reached his horns back until the ivory tips touched his butt. He was a sinister looking devil with his lip curled at Ken as if mocking and trying to smell him. Fortunately, Ken had the wind in his favor. He extended the legs of his rifle's bipod, got into a sitting position and fired his .338 Winchester Magnum.

Ken hit the bull with a frontal shot that required a follow-up. He hit the elk again and knocked him down for the second time. The powerful bull required yet another shot before he succumbed to his wounds. When the elk was down for good, several hunters drove by for a look at him. The hunters helped Ken load the big elk into his truck for the ride home. He pulled into Buttrey's Supermarket, where Toni worked as a cashier. Everyone thought he had poached the bull because the normal elk season was still 14 days away, but he had licenses to prove that he hadn't. With a trophy elk in his pocket, Ken concentrated on big deer for 1985 and '86.

In 1985 he picked an area that wasn't difficult to hunt and harbored lots of deer after talking to game wardens. He held out for a bigger buck, figuring a young buck wasn't worth the work. He only saw one big five-point that cleared a fence and disappeared into the timber. Ken was left dumbfounded, but with a better respect for the intelligence of a large mule deer buck.

In '86 Ken hunted on the Platte Ridge of Snowy Range because it was a better region for big mule deer bucks. The problem was that those deer were more like whitetails in that they rarely left the timber. Usually deer left the timber at twilight or first light. This part of the Platte Ridge was also home to a good population of bighorn sheep. They had been transplanted there in the 1970s by Wyoming's Game & Fish wardens. Ken remembered the terrain when he hunted sheep back in the 1970s when his wife had a permit. On those hunts they recalled the sight of several huge mule deer made his finger twitch. Now in 1986, he would actually hunt them.

Ken picked quite a rocky drainage to seek out a trophy deer. Friends had accompanied him, so transporting a deer would be easier. He walked slowly and spent more time watching than exerting himself. His heart started running as before. While moving very slowly, he sat on a rock where he noticed a dark form above him on his second day of hunting.

He quickly focused his binoculars to find an immense three-point staring back at him. Quickly, he sat behind his bipod-supported .257 Roberts and aimed it with a two by seven riflescope. The shot downed the biggest bodied deer Ken had ever taken; another animal to confirm Ken's knowledge that he had recovered from his heart attack of 1982.

He invited his heart surgeon, James Byrne, to hunt antelope with him the following year. Ken knew a ranch west of Laramie that needed three more hunters that fall. Ken, Toni, and Dr. Byrne obtained permission to hunt antelope easily in Wyoming due to their large numbers. They left early that morning in September of 1987 in search of respectable antelope bucks.

Dr. Byrne had the first shot since he was the guest. Light barely started painting the eastern sky when Ken spied a decent buck on top of a moderate ridge. The silver-haired host drove around to the front of the buck and let Byrne walk out behind the animal.

"Just take your time, Doctor," said Ken before driving away. "We'll hold his attention until you can get a shot."

Dr. Byrne slowly climbed the bank, cradling his .270 Weatherby Magnum. The hosts played decoy by driving out in front of the antelope, which held his attention, but didn't threaten him. It all worked magnificently as Byrne sneaked to within 100 yards and dispatched the distracted antelope. Toni was second to fill her license with a decent buck. She had executed a skillful stalk to take a 125 yard shot. Ken was last to bat when he found a small herd drinking water at a well. Toni drove the two hunters close enough so that Ken could make a stalk. He found a wash that took him to the herd he sought. Two dominant bucks ruled the bunch and traded sparring jousts after quenching their thirst. Ken found the draw very accommodating and cut his shooting distance significantly. He crouched down and poked out of the arroyo when he felt the time was right. The bucks were within 300 yards and quite distracted by the flirtatious does. Ken poked his 6mm Remington forward, supported by the bipod once again. It took one shot and the biggest male of the herd fell. Each of them had all tagged trophy bucks but Dr. Byrne had the largest one by fractions of an inch.

In 1988, Dr. Byrne again accompanied Ken and Toni on a hunt for deer and antelope to a familiar region of The North-Medicine Bow Mountains. Dr. Byrne was more than interested in hunting by this time and had a safari to Africa planned. The antelope sector was just northeast of Laramie, so they could hunt near Ken's home. They turned to antelope first and filled their tags on opening morning. From Laramie, they hunted along the Medicine Bow River where big bucks were present but sparse. When they drove to the spot, Dr. Byrne and Ken split up to cover more ground. Toni tagged along with Ken and carried her .308 rifle. The three hunted all morning and rejoined company for lunch.

"Where do you think we can find these bucks?" asked Dr. Byrne while munching a sandwich. "We've covered a lot of ground."

"These Snowy Range deer are all timber hugging critters," replied Ken, twisting his neck to stretch. "Either we sneak up on them while they're in the timber or wait until they come out, tonight."

They used both strategies, though finding a deer mired in thick brush and trees was harder than it sounded. Ken knew that an animal had every advantage with its superior senses in thick cover. That was probably why more mule deer and bighorn sheep stuck to the trees to survive heavier hunting pressure. Their luck finally turned. As Ken was walking a ridge line, he saw a white spot below at the edge of some aspen. Those white butts gave away more mule deer than any other feature. Ken set up his 6mm Remington and pointed it almost straight downhill. The distance was 300 yards so he held low due to the steep angle. The big three-point was dropped with a shot to the spine. They rejoined later for the long drag back to the vehicle. By the time they arrived, a slender moon gave little light to help them.

In 1990, Ken started feeling ill again. After tests he learned that he had developed more life-threatening heart restrictions. Though Ken carried some weight, he was in the best shape of his life. He learned that these blockages were hereditary. He worked on a local ranch doing chores such as loading haybales and fixing fences, to keep active and to avoid putting on weight. Ken and Toni went back to Wichita to have Dr. Byrne do the operation once more. This time, Ken had a better disposition about the risky procedure, having already been through the surgery once. Dr. Byrne performed five bypasses to rehabilitate the failed organ. Ken was in surgery for nine hours but was back on his feet as quickly as before. This time, Ken and Toni stayed at Dr. Byrne's home after surgery. He returned to his walking program to maintain the shape he had acquired on the ranch and recoup from surgery.

It wasn't long before he could return to Laramie. Since the operation was done on December 4th, he had plenty of time to recover before hunting season arrived. He was anxious to return to his ranch chores, although he would later retire form the job due to his age. Ken stayed long enough to help with calving that spring though he was actually pushing his recovery. Still he planned an elk hunt in a limited quota area near his home that fall.

Ken hunted north of Laramie in the Laramie Mountains with a friend, Tim, that fall for trophy bull elk. Both hunters had drawn a limited permit for the sizeable region. Ken found permission to hunt from a landowner who had let him hunt antelope in the past. He picked up Tim that morning, well before dawn.

It was mid-October and the morning was crisp, perfect for hot coffee. They drank much of the brew before the hunt. They split up to work a draw from different directions, having a hunch that some elk lay in there. When Ken came around a rock, an awesome sight waited for the veteran hunter. He had an eight-point bull elk hiding in that canyon and he sighted it at 300 yards with his .338 Winchester Magnum. He waited for Tim to shoot, feeling that he had a better shot. But Tim couldn't see the bull that Ken was pointing at. In hindsight, Ken probably should have hammered the bull. A Monarch elk doesn't leave the window of opportunity open for long. The monster slipped around some rocks and was gone before either of them could fire. Any elk hunter knows that there isn't much use in following a spooked elk. The chance had come and gone, leaving both men cussing and scratching their heads. Ken was glad for the grand welcome home from bypass surgery though most sportsmen will never see an eight-point bull elk.

Many people undergo heart surgery but refuse to attempt the vigorous outdoor activity that is a part of Ken's life. He hasn't let the uncertainly, doubts and fear stop him from the sport he savors the most, hunting.

Ken Hall displays his six-by-six bull elk he ambushed amid the swamp of Rock Creek near Arlington, WY. Hall dreamt about taking such an elk while hospitalized after a heart attack.

Chapter 9
Peace of My Mind

Driving in Germany is dangerous. Anyone who has been over there can tell you why. Roads are often narrow with some places ill-marked and weather conditions can be hazardous.

We were celebrating 3/7th Cavalry's successful Annual General Inspection at the Officer's Club at Conn Kasserne in Schweinfurt, Federal Republic of Germany on December 1st, 1978. A group of Lieutenants had gathered to watch the annual Army-Navy football game via Armed Forces Network.

"Looks like Boat-U is gonna kick butt again," said Bob Porter, Alpha Troops executive officer. "Maybe we ought to find another diversion for a Friday night."

"I've heard of a disco up at Rannugan where we might find some diversions," said Lieutenant Allen McCord of the 703rd Maintenance Battalion.

"Let's go," said Stew Moss, 3/7th Cav support platoon officer pointing to the door.

We needed two cars because McCord's Volkswagen Beetle couldn't hold us all. Stew followed Allen in his Plymouth Duster accompanied by Alpha Troop platoon leader Jim Carlin. There were few frauleins at the disco, however, so we decided to have some beers and wonder back home. Al led with his Volkswagen, but wasn't prepared for local rain that had left icy patches on the road. When we drove over one such spot, the Volkswagen slid off the road and into a tree. While Bob and Allen suffered superficial injuries, I lay in the backseat unconscious from a blow to my right temple. The bug was without seatbelts, leaving me to bounce violently against the side window. Stew and Jim arrived quickly to administer first aid and go for help.

When I arrived at the Third Infantry Division Hospital in nearby Wurzburg, doctors immediately flew me to Second Army General at Landstuhl just outside of Frankfurt, FRG. I was hospitalized there for over one month. My best friend in Schweinfurt, Lieutenant Joe Baker, was designated to look after my affairs due to my injury. When my younger brother flew to Frankfurt from the Naval Academy in Annapolis, Maryland, Joe met him at the airport. Joe and my brother prepared my flight to Fitzsimons Army Medical Center in Denver, Colorado 100 miles from my hometown of Cheyenne, Wyoming.

The next six months included evaluations, therapy, convalescent leave, and vocational rehabilitation. I was in serious shape with partial paralysis, decreased mental functions, aphasia, etc. The Army concluded that I should be medically retired in July, 1979.

I returned to the care of my parents after my retirement and then the real rehabilitation began. During my convalescent leave, Dad talked me into developing my own physical rehabilitation program. Progress was rapid during the first year after my injury, but then it slowed and was complicated by mental problems. I endured much frustration and subsequent depressions in the attempt to continue my social life and my dream of pursuing journalism. Mental turbulence continually set me back, but I continued to battle on. I refused to quit and be ruled by the stern limitations placed on me by that wreck in Bavaria. Construction projects, swimming, bowshooting, and occasional outings nudged me toward recovery. I was vulnerable to stress from individuals and situations. People perceived me as being dim-witted or uncouth. My delicate mental balance was easily upset by mildly complex events.

During the fall of 1979, I accepted an invitation to go rabbit hunting with a friend in Sybille Canyon, 80 miles from Cheyenne. I paired up with my buddy, Gabe Flores, while his two brothers each invited a friend. Andy Flores and Dan had the best luck as they were the most aggressive hunters of the group. I hadn't seen one rabbit at the end of the day and rode home sulking to Cheyenne in the Flores' brother's International.

"I didn't even see a bunny, man," said Chris Flores as he drove south. "How'd you two find those rabbits?"

"Hey guy, you're looking for the wrong kind of bunny, said his brother Andy, laughing. "We should have left you back in Cheyenne for as well as you hunted today."

Andy always had a crude sense of humor, and was the most outspoken of us. Chris' pal, Mike, rushed to his defense.

"Chris has a lot on his mind, Andy, just like Bill here." He looked at me. "He hasn't said anything all day."

"I can't find any kind of bunny," I replied.

My hunting skills were not the only abilities stripped from me by the car wreck. I had become withdrawn. Most of my post-Fitzsimons hunting was unsuccessful and not very therapeutic. Before I entered the military, I spent the entire fall of 1977 hunting professionally. Outfitter L.D. Frome of Alfton, Wyoming hired me on as a mule deer guide. Hunting was my love and profession. After guiding 15 hunters to their mule deer in Grey's River country, I couldn't accept the aimless wandering that had become my hunting method after my accident. Nonetheless, I continued my pursuit of game that fall. College friends invited me on a bowhunt early that fall in nearby Snowy Range. Mark and Liz Lord had hunted with me in my final year at the University of Wyoming. They visited me while I was at Fitzsimons and were anxious to see me act like the old Bill again. We tried our hand at deer and elk near the summit of the Medicine Bow Mountains. They left me to hunt on my own, as they were accustomed to hunting as a pair.

Wandering around the forest like a sleepwalker, I didn't have the confidence to go very far from camp. While I struggled with my recent past, the couple saw big game, but were hampered by the limitations of a bow and were unsuccessful as well. But at least they were seeing game, while I saw only squirrels, birds, and ghosts. Other hunts were scoreless for me as well that year.

I hunted these same mountains with a rifle accompanied by my father's friend, Ray. Another fellow completed our hunting party and we all slept in Ray's trailer. Ray and his friend, Bill, were seeing game, but I was bothered by gray squirrels agian.

"Got a shot at a lone cow this evening but my eye couldn't focus on her," Ray said excitedly while he peeled carrots for stew that evening. "This darned eye needs to be fixed."

Ray had arrived at retirement age and was being plagued by health problems, like so many seniors. His eyesight was failing him, as were his hearing and his memory.

"We should've been with you," Bill said to Ray. "Seems like the elk stay away from hunters that can shoot."

"Hell, Ray can shoot," I defended grinning. "Problem was he didn't start off the day with a shot of Jack Daniels."

We finished the weekend hunt with no elk, but at least one of us had a shot. That's better than a lot of weekend hunters do.

Antelope waited for me in a huge area near Gillette, Wyoming the next week. My bowhunting buddy, Mark and I opted to apply for the most successful area for trophy antelope in Wyoming. We designated an alternative area near Gillette, Wyoming, just in case we should not draw our first pick. We didn't.

It was a long drive to Gillette. We took two vehicles as Mark's brother, Barry, came with us. I drove with Mark's pretty wife, Liz, to the distant area. The country southwest of Gillette is as flat as the maps we used to navigate the area. Most of the land was private, so we stopped often to ask permission for landowners. Needless to say, attaining permission on the spur of the moment is always difficult. Mark and Barry would drive up to a rancher's home, flashing their out-of-state license plates and wearing shoulder-length hair and they weren't successful ever once in getting permission.

When I drove up with my Wyoming licensed truck, still sporting a military haircut, and with Mark's wife at my side, few landowners would refuse. We had lunch that noon, laughing at our attempts to get permission. I explained to the brothers why they were having difficulty, it wasn't too many months before Mark was sporting a new haircut and driving with Wyoming plates. Mark was serious about hunting the West. That first afternoon, Liz and I spied antelope near an operating oil derrick.

"I think we can get near those goats over there." Liz pointed near the well. "I'll think we'll be far enough from those men."

"Let's try it," I agreed. "I'm tired of riding around this area."

We maneuvered the truck closer and then proceeded on foot. There was a berm between us and our quarry that concealed our short stalk. Nearing the rise, I turned to Liz, pointing.

"Let me go forward to the top of the rise so we don't spook the antelope," I said. "Those antelope don't need to see both of us."

"I'd like to watch but it's you're shot," she said brushing her long dark hair from her eye. "Hope Mark and Barry are seeing antelope over where they went."

I duck-walked slowly to the small berm, dropped into a prone position and crawled forward. The three bucks were busy eating, turned away from me toward the oil well. Some men working at the well were watching my final approach. I slowly worked my bolt-action rifle and sighted through the scope. The goats were only 200 yards from me. They weren't the trophies we had hoped for, but given that this was a non-trophy area, they were the best we might come up with.

Pushing the safety off, I sighted on the largest one and squeezed the trigger. It was a humane kill with the animal dropping in his tracks. I could see workmen pointing from the oil well, waving their arms as I dressed by buck. Right away, I became concerned that we were hunting where we weren't supposed to. We loaded the carcass and drove to meet our companions, miles away. I couldn't help by express my fears to Liz.

"What do you think those workers were pointing at?" I asked worriedly. "You don't think that we were hunting too close to that well?"

"Those guys were just excited that you killed that antelope," Liz said, "If you had done something wrong, they would have us by now."

"I hope you're right," I said still doubtful. "They may have seen our license plates and called the authorities."

"For what?" she answered, irritated. "They were just workers and can't care less about a legally taken antelope."

"But why were they pointing?"

"I told you why," she said, exasperated. "I was so proud of you, making that stalk and shot just like the old Bill. You have nothing to worry about."

When we joined up with the other hunters, we found that they had been successful as well. Their thoughts about the oil workers on the oil rig mirrored Liz's. It took several days before I could stop worrying about my buck antelope. Liz called me a worry-wart, because I fretted about everything. I would spend sleepless nights, thinking about all types of concerns, most of them ridiculous. When something valid attracted my attention, I would go into conniptions and spend much time without sleep.

My hunting year ended with a post-Christmas elk hunt near Grand Teton National Park in Northwest Wyoming. One of my college roommates, Greg Keffer, was studying at medical school in Omaha, Nebraska. When Greg had time over Christmas break, he talked me into hunting near Grand Teton National Park in Wyoming for elk.

Temperatures in Jackson Hole sunk to 22 degrees below zero. We camped at Pilgrim Creek trail head where the mercury dipped even lower. We had never hunted the drainage before but with two horses to buck snowdrifts, we were brave.

I was of little help to Greg in my weakened condition and with the elements being as nippy as they were, I was even worse. Greg was no racehorse either, but our third day of hunting brought us new luck. I found a huge six-point bull that was sunning himself in a snowy basin below our packed trail. We used poor judgment in trying to harvest the bull.

"How in the world are we going to sneak on him in that hole?" I urgently whispered to Greg. "Every approach is either snowbound or in his eyesight."

"Let's shoot from here," he said, confidently. "Both our rifles shoot pretty flat."

We timed our shooting but long distances put limitations on most riflemen. We couldn't see the bullets impact with the snow-cover, so we couldn't ajust fire. After about eight rounds, the monarch slowly rose and walked over the ridge. It was the biggest bull elk either of us had ever shot at and it had just walked away. We were silent for several minutes.

"Those were awful long shots," Greg said finally. "Maybe we should have tried to get closer." He paused. "But maybe it's a good thing that we didn't get that bull."

"We sure would have earned that elk," I added, knowing just what Greg meant as I pondered my weakened condition.

We hunted for two more days with no results, as few elk remained outside the National Elk Refuge. Due to Greg's schooling, we had hunted too late in the season. Between the harsh weather we faced and Greg's psychology, I returned from the trip standing a little taller. We drove back home where I started junior college at Laramie County Community College.

I enrolled in just two classes at the urging of my father. He knew a stiffer course load would send me back to the hospital. I tried working on the student newspaper, but found that the extra curricular work plus school was too taxing. I spent many nights sleeplessly worrying about school, so when spring turkey season came, I was more than ready. Unfortunately, my mind was not.

Probably the most therapeutic hunt that I experienced was the turkey trip I embarked on with Randy and Liz. Liz was having trouble accepting her divorce and I was wallowing in confusion over school. Randy was a Vietnam veteran, several years older than Liz and I were, and he was able to bring us out of the shells we had retreated into. We all saw several turkey on the hunt but couldn't get the drop on them. The three of us cemented a friendship that made the hunt secondary. We all argued as to who had the best time on the trip.

I spent the summer of 1980 working on my family's home-remodeling project, swimming, and bowshooting to prepare myself for the fall hunting season. I would have attempted college again to recover my misplaced academic skills, but I was fortunate enough to draw a Wyoming moose hunting license for Grey's River, near Afton, Wyoming in late September. The fall of 1980 would be a turnaround from the way I had hunted the year before. My first test occurred on a ranch west of Cheyenne I had decided to hunt with my bow and arrow.

Early September was hot that year so I was lucky to draw an antelope area close to Cheyenne where we could process the meat quickly. Our neighbor accompanied me on those daily trips to the ranch, 12 miles from town. Rich would plan an ambush at one waterhole while I did the same at another. We spent days waiting, missing shots, and wondering how we could be so incompetent with our bows. Rick had just undergone back surgery, giving him much to contemplate just as I had. Just getting out of the house was therapy enough for us. The hunting method was ideal for Rich with his back problems.

My lack of movement and the midday heat must have been enough to coax antelope to the stock-tank. A gurgly snort woke me to three animals partaking of the water.

Slowly rising at the sound, I faded behind the windmill legs. I drew the bow slowly, but one of the animals spotted movement and broke into a run. The other two antelope were slower and stopped as I released an arrow toward the closest prairie ghost. It was a solid hit that drove the goat to jump a few steps and expire. I felt great, even though the antelope sported just nine-inch horns. Confidence flowed in me again and I was excited to know that Grey's River awaited me.

I had timed the hunt to coincide with the elk-rut as well as moose. When I found no one confident to hunt with, my father closed his barber shop for a week to be with me in Grey's River. If he had not come, I probably would have let the moose permit lay idle having found no other help. My antelope hunting buddy, Rich, decided to pitch in with us at the last minute, as did a retired neighbor. We drove two vehicles across the state of Wyoming. When we pulled into the long Wyoming drainage, we could see and hear elk rutting on the hillside across the river from where we camped. But first we would concentrate on moose, and then turn to elk if time allowed.

It might have been the moose-rut too, but all the animals were hidden in the deep timber. Dad and I combed the valley for days and only had one fleeting glimpse of a cow moose. We had rented horses for the excursion, and they proved invaluable in hunting the drainage. We were able to ride a lot of country, but those timber-hugging moose wouldn't give us a shot.

When I hunted with Rich, my luck changed. We were driving through a valley called McDonnal Gap when Rich's sharp eyes spotted a young bull at timber's edge, uphill from us. There were two hills to give us cover for our stalk. Hugging the hillside, we eased closer to the quarry. When I had closed to within 250 yards, I slipped into a prone position, using a log for support. I breathed slowly, nostrils inhaling the aroma of the sap from a nearby spruce.

The valley echoed the shot as the bull stumbled forward and went down. We raced forward and Rich checked the animal to make sure it had expired. With about 500 yards of packing to get the moose to a road, we opted for the horses and made the drive to camp in short time. Dad returned to the hillside with me and the horse to dismember the moose for the pack out.

Locating the young bull had taken us all week, making an elk hunt out of the question. We returned to Cheyenne with enough tender moose-meat for everyone. In just a few weeks and I would be heading for the summit of the Sierra Madre Range with my friend, Randy, to hunt for mule deer. We joined with Randy's fellow National Guardsman, Kirk, to make a deer-hunting trio that weekend. Driving up to the Sierra's, after work on Friday, we met Kirk in a bar in the logging town of Encampment, Wyoming. The area was open for any deer, prompting a discussion about our selectivity that night in the bar.

"What type of deer are you looking for?" asked Kirk, while sipping a beer.

"Being that we can shoot anything up here," answered Randy. "I'm going to shoot the first big animal I see."

"Guess that means that we're going to be meat-hunting," I added, somewhat disappointed.

"Can't eat them horns," finished Randy.

Randy Hirsch and I had always given each other a lot of grief. Randy had served with the Marines during Vietnam. The Marines versus the Army was one source of our kidding, and noncommissioned officers versus commissioned officers was another. We argued back and forth while driving to the summit of the Sierra Madres, an area with which Kirk was familiar. We camped below the road, right under Bridger Peak, the highest mountain in the range. The peak still loomed 2500 feet above us.

We clearly were not out to beat anyone with the deer season being near its end. We were starting a bit late in the day, too, with the sun starting to brighten up the eastern sky. Kirk went up one ridge while Randy and I went up another, straddling the uplift. We climbed until we were right under the mountain's summit. I lost Randy while stopping to glass some slopes below. A strange feeling came over me and I knew that something was there. I scanned and looked, picking apart every tree, bush, and boulder-field.

The sound of rifle fire came from the opposite side of the ridge, then I saw bucks leaping away. Randy's second shot dropped his buck, then I leveled down on mine. My trigger squeeze was crisp, and the second buck dropped near the first. This was the second time Randy and I had successfully teamed up on mule deer.

Dragging those deer down to the truck was the real story of that hunt. It took all three of us three days to get both mulies off Bridger Peak and to our truck. We soon understood why those bucks were hanging out up where they were. They were the hardest earned deer I had ever harvested or been associated with. Randy's deer was a clean 24 inches wide between the antlers, and mine slightly less. They both weighed in at over 220 pounds apiece.

It probably took us longer to drag the deer down because I still I didn't have all of my strength back yet after that car wreck of almost two years earlier. It doesn't take long to get hurt, I had learned, but it sure takes time to recover. I was still in a daze most of the time, almost as if I were intoxicated. Time would eventually erase this feeling but my seemingly permanent buzz was a good reason to avoid liquor. We stopped at the same bar in Encampment to celebrate our success. I drank a soda.

It wasn't until the next spring, in 1981, before I could practice my hunting skills again. I hadn't taken a turkey since 1976. Turkey hunting had always been an obsession for me. With the turbulent weather in Wyoming during April, hunting the sly birds can sometimes be an exercise in fortitude. I secured permission to hunt Wyoming's National Guard training grounds at Guernsey in 1981. My normal hunting buddy, Randy, was somewhat less than enthusiastic about hunting birds, so my father and my cousin, Marty, accompanied me in early April.

Preseason scouting always increases your odds of success and I had several members of the Wyoming National Guard giving me information about turkey whereabouts. I quickly chose to hunt a series of gulches on the training area. We left early for the area on the eastern boundary of Camp Guernsey. Arriving as the light was starting to appear, Marty and I left the vehicle for an adjacent ridge where I would locate turkey with my cedar-box call.

"Gobble-obble-obble," I sounded with my voice after I was answered by a reluctant tom. I turned to my eager dark-haired cousin. "Let's narrow the distance."

We picked up and moved 200 yards in the direction of the boss tom. Again I invited the tom with my box-call. When he gobbled back we realized that he was close, and chose not to move again. The tom and I traded calls until he stopped moving our way. I yelped, clucked, purred, and even gobbled, but the male bird had shut up.

Marty broke the silence with a whisper. "What now?"

I shrugged, not knowing what we should do. The silence continued; we dared not move again. After half an hour, I decided to break contact.

"Let's try the next draw, Marty," I whispered. "There seems to be a lot of turkey here."

It was midday as we moved through the next gully with no success. Deciding to break for a few hours, we readied for the evening hunt. The same ridge line where we had success calling was to be our starting point for that afternoon. Experience had taught me that birds would be vocal in moving to their evening nesting trees, or roosts.

Walking to the top of the ridge, we began calling as we followed the uplift. About 200 yards into our hike, a tom answered and the race was on. Once again we narrowed the distance until we approached shotgun range. A few putts on my call and turkeys began investigating the strange company. When the lead gobbler peaked out from behind a bush, he met a load from my Winchester 1200 shotgun. Marty was close enough to see the shot and rejoiced in my good fortune.

I concentrated on school again that fall, with disastrous results, and didn't hunt again until 1982. I participated in too many activities and became overloaded. My brother Reuben, Marty, and I formed an antelope-hunting trio during Labor Day Weekend that year.

I had had my fill of just putting meat in the freezer. I wanted a nice buck to adorn my wall that year. We opted to hunt a familiar area northwest of Rawlins. We drew lots for the first shot, with my luck prevailing. Riding shotgun through the area, it wasn't long before my eyes set sight on a goat worth investigating.

"How 'bout that buck at starboard, that's right for an Army man," joked Reuben, himself a new Marine officer. "Why don't you look him over?"

"Already am," I said. "He sure looks good. I'd guess him at 15 inches."

Reuben stopped long enough to spill me from the truck, and I quickly found a draw that would afford me good concealment from my prey. I crawled the last few yards to get into a good position for the shot. The .25-06 I carried was my favorite rifle, made for the long distances often required by antelope. Moving to within 250 yards, I eased up on a rock ledge, aimed, and fired. It couldn't have been more simple.

Reuben and Marty were also successful, with Reuben shooting the bigger buck. We loaded the animals and headed for Cheyenne, where I called on my favorite hunting buddy, Randy, for a deer hunt near Saratoga, Wyoming.

Having had good success in the Sierra Madres, Randy and I returned to Bridger Peak for the October 1st opening day. We saw a good buck along the road going into the area but saw nothing on Bridger Peak. We put our heads together for a strategy session.

"What do you think, Randy?" I asked the tall guardsman. "Wanta stay or head over to Sybille?"

"Sybille sounds okay," replied my friend. "Besides, you can shoot any deer in Sybille and that's something that you can't do over here."

We loaded and pointed my truck east toward the rocky canyon country of Sybille Canyon, north of Cheyenne, a place where we had been successful before. It wasn't long after we started when Randy spotted a deer running near the road.

"Hey Bill, there's a deer running over here," hooted Randy. "It's a buck. You better get ready."

I unzipped my rifle case, holding three shells to feed my hungry .25-06 rifle. At the right time, Randy stopped the truck, and dumped me out. I scrambled to get away from the road. I loaded the rifle, aimed, and while swinging the rifle offhand, fired. The bullet made a resounding "whop" as it hit the deer. I don't like taking running shots at animals, but sometimes you have to take what is offered. The buck required a coup-de-grace shot before I dressed him. He was just a yearling two-point, good eating.

I took a lot of flack from Randy about my lucky buck.

"So you never had a lucky buck, Lieutenant," Randy teased, remembering that I had just stated that fact minutes before. "What do you do for an encore?"

"Sometimes when you talk, you end up eating crow," I admitted, laughing while I dressed the young deer. "This buck ought to be pretty good eating too."

Hunters in Wyoming are fortunate in that they can practically hunt state-wide for elk, practically until year's end. My success hunting elk near home was nil, so I chose to try my luck near Jackson Hole around December 1st. I was invited by an outfitter friend, Bob Lowe, to hunt with his friend, Terry, out of Jackson Hole. I traveled there after Thanksgiving, racing a winter storm that threatened the region. The sky was clear until I drove down Togwotee Pass on my way to Jackson Hole. The further I drove, the bigger the flakes became until I pulled into Terry's house in Jackson. I walked in the door to find the elk hunter disgusted with pursuing the critters. He told me about the local elk hunting.

"Hate to tell you this, but the main elk herd is already in the refuge," said the stocky, blond outdoorsman. "Don't know if it would be worth trying to locate a late migrating elk."

I shrugged. "Well, what are my options? I drove all this way to hunt.

"They're having an elk-depredation hunt down at Afton, I hear," replied Terry. "Maybe you can hook up with someone down there."

I rested at a local cafe and had an early dinner that evening before negotiating the road south to Afton. My best friend in Afton was a man who had guided with me years earlier when I hunted deer in Grey's River. Randy Schmoker was happy to see me when I unexpectedly pulled into his driveway in Afton during a snow flurry. He and his best friend, Brad, greeted me outside as I strode for the door.

They welcomed me inside and invited me on an impromptu elk hunt. I stayed with the Schmokers for the next week while we pursused elk in the Salt Range above Afton.

Everyday was an adventure, bucking the two foot snowdrifts while looking for elk. The strategy was simple. We would spot elk with our high powered optics from Highway 89 which connected Star Valley to the rest of the world. After spotting elk, we would plan our move and execute the final stalk on foot after tying up our horses. Bulls were few on this hunt. Wyoming's Game & Fish Department had tagged this a depredation hunt to thin elk herds that were bothering ranchers' winter hay. My short legs left me at a disadvantage in negotiating the high snow. Randy and Brad were stalking the elk before I could ever see them. However, due to rifles battered in the rifle-scabbards, my friends were missing shots. Randy harvested the first cow on the second day of the hunt, after we had resighted their guns.

Each day Randy would mush his sled-dogs to get them in shape for the coming winter. One evening, the city fathers had us mush Santa Claus and his three lovely elves into the town square, so that the town's youngsters could get in their requests for Christmas.

Another night, Randy and I were alone with seven dogs pulling the sled down a country road. We could see a vehicle about 500 yards ahead. The distance closed and this vehicle failed to give us the right-of-way, but we expected it to turn at any time. My eyes were transfixed by the approaching headlights until he decided that this car was not to be deterred.

"Jump, Bill!" yelled Randy while he gave the sled a shove into the ditch with all his might.

The headlights kept coming as I sat glued in the basket. The lead dog turned but the second and third dogs were not as lucky. The car's driver hit the brakes, sending it sliding into the ditch, pinning me and the sled underneath. It seemed to happen in slow motion. I was the sliding car swinging towards my body. I closed my eyes, waiting for the pressure to come, and then it stopped. Randy's powerful shove probably saved my life.

"Bill!" he shouted. "I thought you were dead."

One of the dogs wasn't so lucky. It was pinned under thousands of pounds of automobile. I'll never forget the expression of the other sled-dogs as they saw and heard their companion die, nor will I forget Randy's frantic digging, as he tried not to be bit by a maddened, dying dog. The other injured dog sustained just a few cuts. A spectacled Aftonite staggered from the vehicle, visibly drunk. Sharp words were exchanged but Randy didn't press the issue, realizing that the man was too drunk to argue. Randy and I walked to his house where we composed ourselves over coffee.

"Many times I become frozen by situations and don't move like I should." I explained feverishly. "I don't know how many times the honk of an angry motorist has snapped me back to reality. Or how many times somebody kept me from walking into something. I'm not the same old Bill and I continually have to adjust for that."

"Anyone can freeze when they see a car coming right for them," Randy said.

I shrugged. "Yeah, but that's not like the Bill of Mink Creek days."

I readied our gear for the next day of hunting.

We tried an area just north of Afton and quickly spotted elk in the hills above. Randy knew an access point where we could unload horses. Up we rode, knowing the general vicinity of our small elk herd. We started to angle across the ridges until we could get a shot at these elk. I rode low, Brad high, and Randy in between. We traversed the steep ridges toward the unsuspecting herd. One more ridge and we would be facing the elk on the next slope. I tied my horse and crept up to the top of the rise.

Three cows were feeding on the next slope with their snouts buried in new snow. The rocks offered me a perfect shooting platform as I eased my seven millimeter magnum over the top. I drilled one of the unknowing cows right through the lungs, and she expired within a dozen yards. Now I had plenty of meat for the winter, having filled three game licenses that fall. Normally I process my own game but with an impending cougar hunt awaiting me in Colorado, I paid someone else to finish cutting my elk. The lion hunt would be my first guided hunt since my accident.

Knee deep snow coupled with murderous terrain aided the cougar, while the hounds increased their lead on us. The mountain lion was treed for the fifth time when I got my first sight of him. He was picking branches so quickly as he ran atop the thick cedar trees that he looked like a ghost running on top. Outfitter Mark Cremeens gave me a shove broke my stupor and got me running again.

"Git up there," pushed Cremeens.

"Don't have much light left," gasped his friend, Jim Pope.

Four hundred miles of driving and four miles of chasing down a cougar in Hunter Canyon are exhausting for anyone in one day after Christmas, 1992. Only the adrenaline pumping through me pushed my body the last 100 yards to the final tree.

I had received the lion guide's telephone call the night before in my hometown of Cheyenne. Fresh snow and the sound of his voice prompted me to load my truck quickly. I left Cheyenne the morning of December 27th, 1982, and drove southwest to Fruita, Colorado. After four days of unsuccessful hunting before Christmas, poor lion hunting weather had persuaded me to spend Christmas at home and pray for better weather to finish my cat hunt.

The 18th of December had been first day of some of the most punishing hunting I had ever done. The Bookcliff Mountains of west-central Colorado are some of the most rugged mountains in the West. The range sprawls eastward from Soldier Summit, Utah to Rifle, Colorado. They are one of the best mountain ranges to hunt cougars in the United States. Many trophy pumas have come from the mountains we were about to hunt.

My physical rehabilitation program paid off when I had to run the tortuous terrain. Swimming, running, and body building were all important components in my rehabilitation effort. These forms of therapy helped me out when we hunted Garvey Canyon that first day.

The young outfitter and myself cut roads and trails in Garvey with a four by four and snow machine. Mid-afternoon found us surveying a lion track crossing the road.

"Kind of old, but if we run it, maybe it'll get hot," Cremeens drawled while he dipped Copenhagen snuff.

"Might not have enough light," I questioned.

"Maybe he's laying down a half-mile ahead of us," differed the short lion guide. "Won't know if we don't run it out."

Cremeens led with two dogs on leashes. Luke was a pretty plott, while Tom, a black and tan, was the outfitter's best dog. We pressed up a wash until the track turned hot. When Cremeens turned the dogs loose to run, we did too. I got separated from Mark while running up the wash. The sounds of the hounds running a cougar caused me to hurry myself while climbing a cliff. I fell four feet off an overhang, wrenching my back. This close call persuaded me to use more caution. Cremeens met me while I was coming back down the cut.

"Caught him up on top." Cremeens pointed to the dogs. "We run out of light."

I grimaced. "Guess we can chalk one up for the cougar."

Jim Pope came with us on the second day as we moved one canyon east to Coal. The track we had followed the night before headed there. Many record-book cougars had been taken in the canyon that lay before us, including the number two lion ever taken with a bow. Coal was mined in the fault during the 1920s and the canyon was dotted with mineshafts.

Physically tough hunting has a way of building a biting hunger in cat hunters. Supper that evening provided us an opportunity to figure out what was going wrong. We had cut five sets of lion track in Coal, but they were all old. Mark's father, Bill, joined the strategy session.

"There hasn't been a moon out lately, so the cats must be moving during the day," Bill surmised.

"Sure," his son added. "It's been so warm lately that the scent evaporates out of the track before sundown. What we need is about four inches of new snow."

Fresh snow increases a hunter's odds of finding a mountain lion. Cougars will sit out a storm and when it ends, they will be hunting, leaving fresh tracks in the new snow.

Weather reports on the radio in our truck told us that no storms were expected until Christmas. We could expect to sunbathe the remainder of my hunt in 40-60 degree weather. Unless we cut a hot track, the odds of us getting a cat were slim. Cremeens had guaranteed my hunt so that if I did not score, I owed him nothing. Unless we got very lucky, we both stood to lose on the hunt. An idea crept up on me that I thought the outfitter would agree to.

"Instead of me staying out my hunt down here, how about if I take a rain check and come back when we get the weather? We might both do good that way."

"Sounds like the thing to do, Bill," Cremeens replied.

Arrangements were made to get in touch with each other after Christmas.

White snow covered the Central Rockies over Christmas. Colorado and Wyoming were being battered by a fierce winter storm, with some areas reporting twenty and thirty inches of snow causing nightmares for many. Bad dreams didn't disturb my sleep, but the night after Christmas, an excited telephone call from a lion outfitter did.

"Why don't you get down here, Bill," said the excited Cremeens. "I think we may have found something."

I started out at six A.M. after preparing to leave the night before. I had loaded my truck quickly in the light of the full moon and the fresh snow excited me as much as the outfitter's call. Nine hours later I was pulling into the Circle-K convenience store in Fruita. Cremeens and Pope met me with five dogs barking in the rear of their truck.

"We found a fresh lion-kill in Hunter Canyon," Jim said. "If the panther is still near it and we can cut a fresh track, we can get him this evening."

"It's a big cat," Mark added with a snuff-permeated grin.

Hunter Canyon was four miles east of where we had hunted days earlier.

We stopped to check tracks quite a bit. The road in the floor of Hunter was covered with coyote, bobcat, and bird tracks. We passed the area of the lion kill when we saw a cougar track crossing the road. We turned the hounds loose after Mark examined the cat prints.

"That cat can't be more than a half mile ahead of us," clamored the lion guide.

It wasn't long before the mountain lion knew that it had dogs on its trail. He abandoned the easy ground quickly and decided to give us a good workout. Knee deep snow made the race even more grueling. The cat quickly cut across Hunter and took the chase down the east side of the canyon. He was rapidly leaving us behind; so were the hounds. We started to play catch-up when the baying of the dogs changed to a steady bark.

"They got the sucker in a tree," Jim panted.

We were all blowing pretty hard after sprinting and struggling over three miles. We could catch glimpses of the hounds out in front of us. We closed in while the cat was treed six different times. The sun was dropping in the West too quickly. When Mark shoved me out of my trance after my first awesome sight of a mountain lion, we had 100 yards to reach the final tree.

There was still enough light when I fitted an arrow into my compound bow. The cougar was 20 yards up in a cedar tree. I stepped to get a clear, quartering shot at the puma. I drew my short bow, aimed, and released. The bow's speed put the shaft through the lungs of the animal. The lion broke branches as he came down out of the cedar.

Outfitters normally leash their dogs before a shot is released. Fading light and the smart cat made Cremeens forego the step. The cougar snatched the first dog it could reach when it hit the ground. Brown, the aggressive plott, got too close. Before the cat could rip the dog's neck, a blue tick named Moose led the four-dog assault that saved Brown's life. The violent attack and damage from the broadhead made the cougar let go. I fitted another arrow in my bow but wouldn't risk another shot in the savage fight that ensued. It didn't matter, however as the cat fell dead within 25 yards. Flashlights aided us as we carried the lion down the steep walls of Hunter. He had taken us on a four-mile race in the Bookcliff Mountains.

We knew it was a good cougar when we carried him to the truck. When I was taking pictures on the truck's tailgate, it occurred to me what I had accomplished. I limped but it was from a fall a few days earlier, not from the head injury I suffered four years before. When I was confined to a wheelchair at Second Army General in Landstuhl, my left arm was so paralyzed that I could only steer the chair in circles with my right arm. My first letters from Fitzsimons to friends were scribbled notes.

The series of frustrations and subsequent depressions that I had been through along my road of recovery, had been chilling. All of those frustrations faded in that moment.

We measured the tom to be six-foot-six-inches and he weighed 138 pounds. We rough-scored him to be 14 5/16ths but after the required 60-day drying period, the Wyoming Game & Fish officially scored him 14 3/16ths. The Pope & Young cougar was a major landmark on my recovery trail.

Bill Padilla surveys his 1982 colorado cougar.
The Pope & Young cat scored fourteen 3/16s.

Padilla with his 1982 "lucky buck" mule deer.

Nineteen-eighty was a stellar year for Padilla. He harvested a young bull moose in Wyoming's Grey's River region.

Padilla, Randy Hirsch, and Liz Mason ham it up on a rehabilitation turkey hunt to Wyoming's Blackhills.

Padilla, second from right, in pre-injury days working in Western Wyoming as a deer guide.

Three blue-grouse fall victim to the author on a deer hunt near Saratoga, Wyoming.

Randy Hirsch and the author harvested two four-point mule deer bucks in 1980.

With a brace of Colorado Canada Geese, the author explored all types of hunting in his struggles to recover.

Another turkey for the bag. The author called-in this gobbler near Newcastle, Wyoming in 1983.

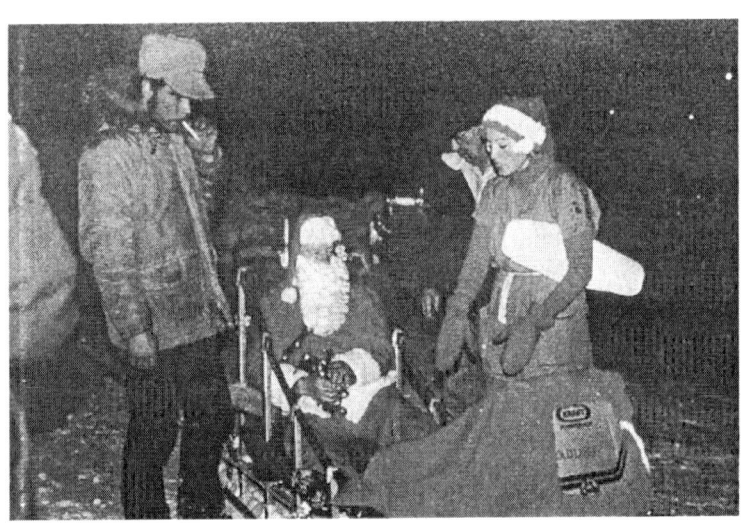

Randy Schmoker transports Santa Clause and his elves after a December Wyoming elk hunt in 1982 with the author. Padilla took a large cow elk on this hunt.

Chapter 10
Stoned

Almost every sportsman would like to have a bearskin rug in his trophy room. Mark Cremeens offered me a chance to hunt for black bear south of Grand Junction, Colorado. I opted to hunt a bruin with my percussion-cap muzzleloading rifle.

We hunted in early June of 1983 in the Uncompahgre National Forest, out of a tent camp. Mark had several bear frequented baits in the surrounding forest. When I arrived in Fruita, Colorado, Cremeens already had a particular bait in mind for the evening hunt.

"So, do you have more than one bear hitting your baits?" I asked as we drove south.

Mark grinned and nodded "I have one bait over a small cliff that's being hit by several," he said. "There's a blonde, brown, and a cinnamon all feeding the last time I checked."

"I'll take any of 'em," I said. "Though I've always been fond of brunettes."

"I like blondes myself," Mark added with a grin.

We pulled into camp around noon. The cook was busy peeling potatoes for that evening's supper. I stowed my duffel, stepped outside, and admired the fantastic scenery provided by Utah's Manti La-Sal mountains just across the state border. It was spring and life was everywhere. Marmots were giving us a comical show in a nearby field of boulders while we were waiting for the evening hunt.

Mark and I took three dogs in the rear of the truck and drove to the cliff where the bears had been striking the bait. Our plans were to watch the bait and hope for a shot off the cliff. If we couldn't get a shot, the hounds were nearby for a chase. We ascended the rocky trail near the site and walked the remainder of the way so as not to frighten off a bear. We snuck our way onto the small cliff, which gave us maximum observation of the approaches from the timer to the bait.

Sitting on a bait for any type of game tests a hunter's nerves. We couldn't talk, kept movement to a minimum, and our readiness to shoot kept us on the razor's edge.

We took turns looking over the edge for a visitor from below. When it was my turn to relax, I thought about the progress I'd made in my rehabilitation over the past four years. I remembered my helplessness while in a wheelchair in Germany, the medevac to the United States, my hospitalization at Fitzsimons, and the role hunting had played in pulling me out of the mess that I had sunk into. Then I thought about the anti-hunting forces that wanted to end bear hunts like the one I was on. All the pro and con arguments, notwithstanding, it is hunters that pay for wildlife conservation through license fees and organizations, not anti-hunters.

Mark's gesture snapped me back to reality. He was pointing to the area below our cliff. I cocked the percussion-cap muzzleloader slowly and peeked over the edge. A beautiful cinnamon-colored bear was busy reversing and dove into the timber. Mark raced for the dogs back at the truck while I donned by fanny pack and waited.

Mark's hounds didn't need any guiding. They headed straight for the bait. An eager plott named Luke put his nose in the bear scent near the bait and led the hounds into the timber after the bruin. We raced after the trailing black and tan hounds as they followed Luke. Off we ran, branches whipping our faces. It wasn't long before the dogs jumped the bear and we were right behind. We could hear the hounds before us.

The bear stopped to fight the dogs in a small clearing. We broke into the meadow to see a hound being hurled across the opening. I shouldered my .50-caliber Hawken replica, recocked and fired. The 500-grain bullet knocked the bear flat. We didn't have a long pack to get back to the truck, but he was certainly a large bear, measuring seven-foot-two in length and 300 lbs. in weight. The cinnamon-colored bear won a black powder award from the National Rifle Association. The large bear fortified my confidence for the thrashing I would endure, in graduate school.

Since my military career was over, I had to formulate another goal for myself. I had become interested in national and international affairs. Advancing that interest would be helped by attaining a masters degree in public administration. I can now look back at the lunacy of it. I had severe trouble passing intelligence tests, so I don't know why I thought I could handle graduate work, nonetheless, I tried.

Stress made me withdraw from graduate school. I turned to an activity that almost always reduced stress—hunting.

By the time spring turkey season came around in April, I had already quit graduate school though I finished out my classes for the semester. Since I only had two days of classes each week, I planned a four-day foray to South Dakota's Black Hills. I had not been successful in drawing a Wyoming turkey license and so set my sights on South Dakota, which issues unlimited licenses for birds in their Black Hills around Rapid City.

I tried to find a turkey-hunting companion but was unsuccessful. I had been to Wyoming's Black Hills several times, and South Dakota being only a few miles from my old haunts. Armed with general hunting information from South Dakota's Game & Fish Department, I resolved myself to try hunting alone in strange country.

The three hundred mile drive went quickly, and I pulled into a Newcastle, Wyoming cafe for a break. It was getting close to the time for an evening hunt, and my area was just a few miles away, across the state line in South Dakota. I had to check the new area out. It was overcast and about 45 degrees, but no rain was predicted. When I exited the highway onto a dirt country road, the forest looked promising. The further I drove, the better the game habitat became. As my truck climbed up the road, I started seeing men busy clearing timber. If anyone knew what was happening there with turkey, those fellows would. When I stopped the third time for information, the woodcutter happened to be a turkey hunter as well. He didn't mind sharing information.

"You fellows have a lot of wood cut," I remarked.

"Just starting," answered the woodcutter. "You look like you are hunting, though."

"Turkey," I answered.

When we finished our discussion, he pointed me toward an opening a few miles away. I drove into the area just as turkey were thinking about heading for the roost. After leaving my truck, it wasn't long before I found tracks and feathers in the mud along a path. I grabbed my .22-250 rifle and scaled a promising trail.

I had read that turkey will gobble when an owl's hoot threatens them. Hooting like an owl wasn't one of my strong points, but I must have done a fair imitation. When I hooted for the fourth time, I received a gobble in response. I followed the sound and kept hooting occasionally, until I intercepted a lone gobbler heading for the woods. I was close enough to dispatch him with a B-B gun, but found him in my scope instead.

I had all summer to prepare for the most exotic hunt I have ever taken. Only through living at home was I able to dream of affording a hunt for stone sheep in British Columbia. The ten-day excursion was expensive in 1984 and was doubled in price since then. The laws of supply and demand govern stone sheep hunting as there are only two places in the world to hunt them—British Columbia and the Yukon. The most beautiful of the wild sheep, everyone wants to hunt them. I had stopped at Laramie Taxidermy when the owner was mounting one from British Columbia. The sheep had been killed in the famous Muskwa River drainage of Northeast British Columbia. The sight of the handsome ram committed me to arrange a hunt.

A friend recommended an excellent outfitter, Lynn Ross, from Pink Mountain, British Columbia. Lynn's outfit had guided hunters to some of the largest stone sheep ever taken. I contacted five other outfitters concerning stone sheep, but quickly settled on Ross. His hunt package was more suited to my budget and desires. I would hunt stone sheep, wolves, and wolverine in early August of 1984.

I had to shape up for the hunt. Swimming was my tune-up that summer. Swimming had figured greatly in my rehabilitation and would get me in top shape for sheep hunting, or so I thought. Later I would find my feet woefully unprepared for the sharp rock in Western Canada. My body could take the climbing and walking, but my feet were rubbed raw by the black shale.

I flew to Fort Saint John, British Columbia via Denver, Seattle, and Vancouver. Lynn's pretty wife, Sharon, picked both me and our camp cook up in Fort Saint John. I was looking for a lost sleeping bag when Sharon approached me at baggage claim.

"Are you hunting with Lynn Ross?" she asked.

"Yes," I replied brightly.

"I figured you must be the one," she said, tossing back her shoulder-length auburn hair. "You were the only passenger to pick up a rifle from baggage. I'm Sharon Ross and this is Gladys. She'll do the cooking for you in the backcountry." Introduction made, we piled into Sharon's Chevy Suburban for the 110-mile trip to Pink Mountain.

The Ross Ranch was framed by a backdrop of Canada's finest mountains. I commented on the majesty of them to Lynn.

He smiled placidly. "Wait till you get back to where you're going if you think this is pretty."

I slept well that night, and was hastily awakened by the sounds of a small pack-train being outfitted by our guides, Gary and Al Dowd. Lynn paired me up with a hunter from Southern Bavaria. Rudy Cherwonka spoke limited English and I spoke even less German, but hunters always have a common language.

I recognized Gary Dowd from a Safari Club International publication. Striding up, I extended my hand. "Bill Padilla, Gary," I said. "Need a hand loading up?"

"How'd you know my name?" said the reddish-blond guide.

"Hell, you're famous," I teased. "You're all over Safari Club publications.

"You bin other sheep hunter?" asked Rudy in broken English.

"That's me," I answered. "*Spreche Deutsch?*"

"No, we practice English," returned the fair-haired German.

"Okay, but I haven't had a chance to speak German since I was in Schweinfurt with the American Army."

"Ah, you were en Schweinfurt den," asked Rudy, smiling. "Vel, ve speak English for sake of the Canadians."

I knew Rudy and I would get along just fine. Five riders and three packhorses took all day to make Halfway River. Ross refused to use airplanes in his hunting concession and that was fine with me. I felt like a hunting guide again, and the country just got better and better while we rode in. British Columbia was the best-looking country I had ever seen.

We pulled into the cabin at about six P.M. that day, and I proceeded to help with camp chores. I wanted to feel like I was contributing to the success of the hunt.

"Sure is nice having an ex-guide around hunting camp," said Al while unsaddling horses.

Gary just smiled while Rudy flashed a look of disbelief. "Vot did you tink of Schweinfurt," asked Rudy while we unpacked.

"I didn't spend much time there to get any kind of opinion," I answered. "We were in Grafenwohr, Hohenfels, and at Coburg more often."

"Ah, Coburg," he said, eyebrow raised. "You must have had border duty."

"Then you know about the United States Cavalry" I asked.

He grinned. "Yes, ve have all seen John Vayne at de cinema."

We both laughed.

Gary was the more experienced sheep guide, though his brother Al was older and had guided for other animals for outfitter Garry Vince. Al continually picked his younger brother for information about the country. This was Al's first year with Lynn Ross. The pair quickly made plans for the first day. Gladys, a Cree Indian, would stay at the cabin to cook while Rudy and Gary headed north and Al led me south. The high rocks looked imposing above us and better suited for goats and sheep than for us bipeds. We rode our horses through overgrown creekbeds and tied up at the highest scrub trees before we hit rock.

"On foot from here," commanded Al while tying up.

"No wonder these sheep are so pretty," I said scanning the grayish-black shale.

"Yeah, they can disappear in these rocks if they're sitting still," said Al slipping on his daypack.

That mountain of black shale was the most jagged country I had ever walked. In many places, every step was a challenge to my dissipated coordination and balance. I felt like I would tumble into the beautiful shale I liked so much. Nice to look at, but hell to negotiate. Had I bit off more than I could chew?

Al stopped, took off his gloves, and scanned the distant grass bench with his binoculars. He waved me closer—he'd spotted some sheep. He screwed his beaten spotting scope into a similarly dented tripod and pulled me closer for a look at the animals.

"There he be," Al whispered.

I crawled up to see a band of sheep who were quietly surveying everything below them from a lofty, grassy perch. The dominant ram was visible to the naked eye but my binoculars and the spotting scope brought him much closer. He was a fine sheep.

"What would you guess he goes?" I whispered while storm clouds gathered in the distance.

"Close to forty," Dowd said, frowning at the gathering storm.

My first sight of a stone sheep and I was looking at a forty inch ram. Sheep are rated by the length of their horns, and forty inches is a milestone in sheep hunting, something a hunter dreams of, hopes for, but never really expects to see unless he has unlimited time and money. The sheep was over a thousand yards away so I knew a photograph was impossible, but I wanted a picture of the situation for my records. I crouched low and maneuvered for the photo.

Al's head turned violently. "Get down," ordered the Canadian in rage.

I dropped back into the dark shale, feeling a little foolish. I had barely moved and those sheep spotted me at over 1000 yards. Tense minutes crawled by while we waited to see what the spooked sheep would do.

"Man, can those sheep see," I lamented.

"Hell, ya's a good silhouette up on this ridge," chastised my guide in his Canadian accent. "Wait, they're coming back. This time we'll put the mountain between us and the sheep."

We slipped down among the rocks, and the walking got more and more treacherous. I followed along at a snail's pace with my heart up in my throat. Right then, I was ready to quit sheep hunting and pursue anything that lived on flat ground.

Al stopped and turned when the climbing required technical climbing gear. As I did the same my foot slipped. As I tumbled downward my mind went blank. I could see my rifle sliding by me and my camera bouncing off rocks near the bottom of the gorge. I reached for a rock and broke my fall before I slid over a vertical drop. A lot of people might have been shaky after I tumble like that, but after what I had been through in my recovery, I just swallowed hard and climbed up. Al retrieved the rifle, which had been battered by the fall. The last sight I had of the camera told me that climbing down to retrieve it would have been folly.

"That camera could have been me," I groaned at Al with my eyebrow raised. "Rifle held up okay, but we're gonna have to check the scope."

"Better call it a day," Al said, while wiping his brow.

Just then, the sky opened up and we were treated to a British Columbia soaking. We both donned rainwear and huddled on a ledge, dipping snuff. So we sat in the rain, less than a thousand yards from a magnificent stone ram, with a rifle that had just done a rocky bobsled run. We could only hope the sheep would be in the same area the next day. I looked down to see another casualty of the shale slope. My binoculars were now broken. At least it wasn't the optics and would only affect the focusing mechanism. I would have to focus manually.

"Do ya think this rain el quit, eh?" Al said, rain pouring from the brim of his hat. "We better start back. The scope's off, maybe."

We crept up the shale to better footing. Being socked in by the clouds, the sheep couldn't see anyway. Every step was a balancing act with the wet rock underfoot. I was cussing the terrain for ending my stalk on the forty-incher. I fell repeatedly, jamming my fingers to catch myself. My feet were starting to ache. This was my first wild sheep hunt and now I knew why sheep hunters were a little bit loony. But I had come too far and invested too much money to quit after the first day.

We both strode up to the other hunters at camp that evening. I lamented over the loss of my camera.

"We watched my camera bouncing off the rocks below," I said, despondently. "I guess I was lucky not to have been killed."

"No, I threw that camera off the mountain," chuckled Al. I explained how I had spooked the big ram by maneuvering for a picture.

Gladys had cooked some moose steaks for us that evening. Moose rates high on any outdoorsman's dinner menu. When Al and I checked my rifle's scope, we found it was just a half inch off. We could have waited out the storm and continued our stalk.

"Ya okay after that spill," Al inquired when he saw me thinking.

I shrugged. "My scope and rifle took more punishment than I did," I boasted. "Good thing we quit, though. That fall took the wind out of my sail."

The two Dowd brothers shared information after supper. Rudy and I did the same.

"We had our glasses on a forty-incher," I said, pantomiming the curl of sheep horns. "What a ram. I fell down a slide and that ended our stalk."

Rudy grimaced when I showed him my battered rifle.

"Ah, is looking like sheep hunter's rifle now, yes," he said while tipping back a glass of good bourbon. "Maybe tomorrow you get 'em."

"I hope he's still there," I said.

After supper we didn't waste much time crawling into our sleeping bags. The northern summer gave us long days to hunt by and shorter nights to recover. The next day Al and I went to the same area in search of our ram. We found sheep in the same area but no legal rams (British Columbia required male sheep to be full curl). The black shale was as jagged as before and my feet were suffering. Shortly before noon I saw something crawling through the rocks.

"That a wolverine?" I asked excitedly, pointing in the critter's direction.

"Naw, just a whistler, I think," replied Al.

"Whistler?"

"Don't know what ya call em down there," Al said while putting up his glasses. "A marmot, maybe?"

I shook my head. "Na, I killed plenty of marmots when I was young."

"You're right," admitted the guide while focusing his binoculars. "He's awful light colored."

"I got a wolverine tag but I don't want to risk a shot with that forty-incher here somewhere," I rationalized. "Hate to pass 'em up though."

We looked on mountainsides, benches, basins, even under rocks but the massive ram had disappeared into the gorgeous, wild country. Walking among the jagged rocks was good for my coordination. I was getting better at negotiating the rugged terrain. We came back in dead tired, with strained eyes. My broken binoculars were tough on me. I swore to always carry a spare pair from then on.

We returned to camp where Rudy was sipping coffee in the small shack Lynn Ross had built, years earlier.

"Did you find 'em, Bill?" asked Rudy.

"Naw, he must have got word that we were looking for 'em, Rudy." I shook my head. "Didn't see anything legal. How did you all do?"

"Ve saw many rams but none gut enough," answered Rudy. "Ve shoot the first ram dat ve see now."

Gary and Al talked it over and they decided to switch mountains. Perhaps it would give us both better luck. Gladys had stone sheep steaks for us that night. Since there was no meat packing facility in Pink Mountain, everyone that hunted in warm weather as us would leave game-meat for the cook. My mouth was watering when we dove into the steaks. We were ready for the next day after that dinner.

The morning wasn't ready for us, though. The sky opened up and halted our hunt for the ram. Gary spent the time reading Leo Tolstoy's *War and Peace*. Al did little chores around camp, Rudy was busy with equipment, and I interrupted them all by eagerly asking hunting questions. I wished that I had brought a book as well and probably everyone else wished I had too.

"*War and Peace*," I said. "That's ambitious reading."

"I've seen it rain up here for days," answered Gary, closing the book.

"Hope not," I continued. "At least Rudy could have shot a sheep. I saw one almost a mile away."

"There's plenty of time left," said Al, flipping back his cowboy hat. "We've found them and sometimes that's the biggest part of sheep hunting."

"I thought I'd get to bring my sheep-meat back home," I complained. "I'll have to stay, fish for Dolly Varden trout and eat as much as I can. This meat is some of the best I've ever had."

"Wait till ya shoot your own," added Gary. "Fresh sheep just can't be beat."

The sheep we had eaten was last year's kill as our hunt was the first of the season. I was curious to know the best time to hunt stone sheep. Gary answered quickly.

"Either now or in October is best," he said. "Lynn only gets six sheep permits a year so you can't over hunt his concession."

"Can't you harvest more sheep than that in here?"

"Oh yeah, but permits are allocated as they have been in the past.

Anyone who has hunted the north country has been confined to a cabin or tent while mother nature renews the earth. We all slept tight; the day off had caught us in need of a break.

We switched mountains the next day. The new mountain was not as rough as the forty-incher's home had been. I saw white specks in the rockiest section of the mountain. On inspection with my binoculars, I confirmed 12 goats in a grassy pocket.

"Too bad I didn't get a goat license," I lamented. "But I don't want to take time from the sheep hunt."

"We could do it," said Al. "We got the sheep located and the goats too."

"Aw, goats don't mean that much to me," I rationalized. "I'd rather take a wolverine or wolf."

Up we climbed. As before, we tied up our horses at the timberline and slipped our hiking boots on. Looking over the south end of the mountain, all we found were the small band of goats. We hiked on to the west side where the mountains opened up into a panorama of some of the best scenery left in North America.

We sat, back to back, surveying the slopes above and below. Wildlife was abundant in these mountains. I spotted stone sheep ewes and lambs. Below them I spotted a large grizzly bear that filled my damaged binoculars.

"Wow, look at this," I exclaimed, nudging Al.

Al nodded. "He's looking for rock rabbits among those rocks."

"Hope he doesn't mistake us for rock rabbits," I said. "I see ewes and lambs on that ridge over there."

"Well, I see rams over here," Al shot back.

I turned slowly so as not to alarm anything Al was looking at. Seventeen rams were alternately grazing and returning to their escape cover in a rocky hole in the side of the mountain. We completely forgot about the grizzly and he didn't bother us. We both faced east, surveying the rams as they grazed and scampered to their hole. They were about 800 yards away. Al set up his spotting-scope to see which rams were legal.

"There's three full-curl rams in that bunch," he whispered, squinting through his spotting scope.

"We only need one good ram," I replied.

Al gave me an uncertain look. "No way we can slip up on them from there. Let's go 'round the mountain and look from that rim on the eastside of the hole."

It was already six P.M. when we started stalking. The walking wasn't difficult, there was just a lot of it. We ran into a caribou calf on the south side of our mountain. He gave us a frightened snort when we got within thirty yards, then scampered off.

"Don't think that calf has ever seen a man before," I thought aloud. "Probably looking for his mama."

By the time we reached the rim we chose to observe from, it was eight P.M. We got down on our hands and knees, everything came into view. I couldn't help noticing the landscape from up high; it was absolutely beautiful. Mountains stretched every direction the eye could see. I would shoot from the prettiest spot on earth I had ever been.

Two hundred fifty yards separated us from the stone sheep.

"Your call, Al," I said. "Which one is a legal ram? They all look good to me."

I was in the prone position with my .25-06 pointed in the direction of my quarry. The sheep had not seen us yet.

"Take the one with a left flare in this horn," commanded Al, clutching his binoculars.

"The one facing us by that rock?" I replied.

"No, the one with his back at us," he whispered.

"The one that just kicked his back leg?" I said, anxiously.

"No, no. The one with his head turned to the left."

"The one quartered-away from us?"

"No, damn it."

"The one with a spot on his nose?" I asked.

"Yeah, yeah. That's him."

Using my daypack for a rest, I lined up on the climbing ram. At the report, he folded neatly, but then fell off a cliff and rolled a hundred yards into a ravine.

"Who says a .25-06 isn't enough gun for sheep?," I said jubilantly.

"I never said anything," Al turned to me and grinned. "Must have been Rudy brought that up."

Al raced down the rocky slope at the base of the cliff like a stone sheep himself. I gingerly picked my way down. On reaching my downed prize, Al looked at me solemnly.

"He's not full-curl," he said gravely, then smiled, "Had ya worried, eh?"

Of course he was full-curl, with his horn dipping below the jaw-line and extending past his nose by an inch.

Al whistled. "Thirty-seven inches." He'd wrapped a steel measuring tape around the horn. "Broke a bit off the horn but it's still attached. Any taxidermist worth his salt can fix that. Eight o'clock and we still have a lot of work left to do."

I gutted the ram while Al worked at taking the head off for a shoulder-mount. We worked feverishly, knowing that it would be a late night.

"We'll leave the hams here and take the rest," he said. "I'll come back for the hams tomorrow."

We descended quickly and traversed the mountain to our patient mounts, still tied where we left them. I was happy to get off my aching feet. The horses didn't need any urging back to the cabin as we gave them their heads and rode them home. We crossed several streams on the way back to the cabin. As we crossed one, I noticed the sheep horns starting to slip from our packhorse's drawstrings. Tired, I leaned over to right them and when I did, my saddle slipped to the side of the gelding's back.

Suddenly, I was riding on the side of the horse, whose nostrils widened. Because I was tired, I hadn't changed my boots and my vibram soles were stuck to the stirrups, keeping me from slipping from the saddle.

Al's eyes widened when he bailed off his mount to come to my aid. We tried to get my feet out of the stirrups while my horse bucked and turned.

"Some hunting guide!" Al yelled in frustration.

"Uncinch 'em," was all I could say as my horse bucked.

Al dangled helplessly from the cinch and finally managed to dump me and the saddle from the crazed gelding's back. I slammed into the meadow, grateful as I watched the bucking horse kick. Al rounded up the confused horse while I recomposed myself.

"Man, that's twice on the same hunt," Al hollered. "Someone must like you."

"Or has plans for me," I uttered, swallowing hard. "Those sheep horns never came off the horse, huh?"

Al didn't say anything, silence being enough commentary on my stupid mistake. We rode into the cabin where Gladys was postponing supper until someone returned.

"Gary's not back yet, eh?," Al questioned.

Gladys shook her head.

"They must have something," I reasoned, dipping snuff.

"Maybe," Al said. He walked off to put away the horses.

Gladys cooked up her usual feast when Rudy and Gary dragged themselves into camp.

"Did he give us a chase," Gary gestured at the stone sheep bobbing behind him in the saddle. "Rudy ended up hitting him five times before he went down."

Rudy was trailing along, exertion painted on his Bavarian face. Now the day was starting to turn dark.

"After dat, ve all deserve a trink," offered Rudy, slipping from his saddle. "I tink von sheep es gut enough."

Our guides took care of the horses while we two hunters admired the stone sheep. Rudy had killed the forty-incher I had spent days chasing. Actually, he was just shy of the milestone forty inches and was broken back on the opposite horn. I had already measured my sheep at 160 Boone and Crockett points, while his went 173 points, if he had not been broken. The circumference of the horns at the base was a massive sixteen and a half inches.

"You've shot yourself a big sheep, Rudy," I said.

"You're sheep es very pretty too," he replied.

"You deserve the bigger sheep, though," I returned. "You've been hunting many more years than I. I noticed that you didn't use your binoculars very much while we were riding in."

"Ven you come to my country, I vill look because I know vat to look for," he explained. "I let dese boys look for me; they know vat to look for."

Rudy was anxious to change his flight arrangements and get back to Bavaria. I opted for the trout fishing in a stream near horsecamp. I also wanted to eat as much of my sheep as I could before returning home. In the end, I changed my flight arrangements as well, returning to Cheyenne after two days of trout fishing. Vancouver Airport was bustling as I pushed an overloaded cart through customs. When I got to Cheyenne, I proudly opened the bag to show my parents the trophy, but found the bag had opened. The sheep skin was lost.

"I lost it," I exclaimed with only my stone sheep horns to show. "I better get on the phone before someone throws it away."

What I had lost was the cape, or facial-skin, that my taxidermist could make into a beautiful trophy. I carried the game bag with me into dozens of places; it could have fallen out anywhere. I called United Airlines, the shuttle bus service in Denver, Cheyenne's Municipal Airport, everyplace I could think of. I called my taxidermist to find out what a stone sheep cape would cost. Charlie related that I might as well hunt another stone sheep because a cape was practically unattainable.

Remembering the hectic shuffle I was subjected to at customs, I called the Vancouver Airport, where I was referred to the lost and found desk. I asked about a grayish animal hide that was wrapped in burlap and jumped for joy when the female clerk said they had it.

My next move was to call United Airlines to see if they could fly it to Denver as lost baggage. I found out that they could but United would have to have someone from the lost and found bring it to them. When I called lost and found desk again, the girl said that she couldn't leave the counter. She was Asian and had difficulty speaking English. I was getting frustrated. I had a valuable animal cape sitting in another country, rotting. In hindsight, I probably could have hired an agent to perform the task for me but as frustrated as I was, my only thought was to fly there and fetch the cape myself.

Flying up to Vancouver, I was mesmerized by the beauty of British Columbia's coastal mountains. There beneath me was the best steelhead fishing, grizzly bear, and mountain goat hunting on earth. When I debarked the Boeing 727 in Vancouver, I made straight for the lost and found desk at the airport. I was greeted by the female clerk who had my cape for me under the counter. This skin wasn't getting out of my hands, again. But I had to stay the night in Vancouver waiting for the next flight to Denver, Colorado.

Padilla rides the ridge where he shot his stone ram from in 1984.

British Columbia's pristine wilderness surrounds the author while he holds his 37" trophy, stone sheep cape taken in 1984. Padilla lost his camera in a fall while hunting sheep and nearly lost his life.

Mark Cremeens tosses donuts over the cliff to attract a bear from his forest lair below. The author hammered a fine bruin with his muzzleloader.

With Wyoming's Teton Wilderness in the background, the author lands a fourteen-inch cutthroat trout in 1984. Padilla and Bob Lowe caught over sixty trout in three days.

Chapter 11
Hunting is Rehabilitation

Every hunter has an off year and 1985 was mine. I didn't draw my antelope area, didn't see a deer all season, and didn't plan enough time for elk. One problem was I lacked a steady hunting partner who could take the time off for a particular species. Randy Hirsch had limited vacation time that fall and though I knew other hunters, they didn't want to hunt with me for reasons I have stated before. I couldn't afford a guided hunt every year, so I waited for the next spring.

New hunting areas excite any outdoorsman, so my plan to hunt near Newcastle, Wyoming for turkey, had me thrilled. Though I had hunted nearby in South Dakota, I never ventured on the Wyoming side. As before, I couldn't find a friend to accompany me on the long drive. And as in 1984 when I hunted South Dakota, I stopped for an early supper in Newcastle before heading to my new hunting area.

The ranch wasn't far from Newcastle, so I made an evening hunt as I had in 1984. I had learned about the area from a fellow turkey hunter in Newcastle who directed me to a likely area. After stopping at the ranch, I searched the south end of one of the fields. It was near a wooded draw where good cover afforded turkey protection. Numerous tracks and feathers told me that I was in the right place. I grabbed my shotgun, slipped into some camouflage and crept into the gully adjacent to the field. It wasn't too long before I found a dozen birds busy with a courtship dance, not far from the field's edge. I snuck closer while they were preoccupied with the ritual. With a latex mouth diaphragm, I clucked out flock-talk at the dancing bunch.

They stopped and began to seek out the new intruder, slowly walking in my direction. When they went behind a hedge row, I had an opportunity to move closer. The group appeared from behind the bushes, well within range of my scattergun, which was already at my shoulder. I remained frozen until a large tom crossed my plane of vision.

I fired, sending the remainder of the flock into flight but leaving one boss tom on the ground. Too bad this turkey hunting area wasn't closer to Cheyenne because I certainly had been lucky here.

I wouldn't hunt again until that July. My taxidermist in Laramie arranged for four of his clients to hunt the Northwest Territories with an outfitter who had a good local reputation. I confirmed that reputation by visiting with a retired game warden in Laramie who had gone with Redstone Trophy Hunts. After making the arrangements, I traveled with Wade, Wally, and Joel for the combination Dall sheep-caribou hunt in the McKenzie Mountains. Wade worked out at the health club I frequented and we'd developed a lasting friendship. I wouldn't have to hunt solo again.

We flew to the Northwest Territories via Denver and Edmonton, Alberta. Our last stop was Norman Wells, where we contracted a helicopter to fly us in to Hugh and Tim MacAulay's Hook Lake base camp. The beautiful country abounded with game—our pilot spotted a huge wolf on our way in. The wranglers at the base camp told us that McKenzie Mountain wolves were the biggest in the world.

We were paired up with guides that first evening. Where I drew the youngest, roughest of the lot, Tony. Wade and I departed with Tony and Hugh to an area that hadn't been hunted in two years.

The Tigonankweine, or Rocks of the Bighorn, were to be our hunting ground. We pitched camp and then rode out into the wilderness. When we stopped to investigate some rocks through our binoculars, another quarry caught my eye.

"That's gotta be a wolverine." I pointed while looking through my binoculars. "Maybe we ought to sneak up on him."

Once again, wolf and wolverine tags were in my pocket.

"I don't know, Bill," said Tony, who was glassing the mountain. "We might scare these sheep over here."

I turned slowly and quickly sighted the band of a dozen sheep that Tony had spotted. Wade and Hugh had left us behind as they were en route to another set of mountains. We took a lot of time to size up these sheep. There were three rams leading the flock. I had read many stories about sheep hunters that were too selective in choosing their trophy, and then went home with nothing at all. I wanted a sheep that had at least a 36-inch circumference around the horn. An acquaintance of mine had just finished hunting with Hugh and held out for a 40 inch ram. He was lucky to go home with a 36 inch ram.

Tony set up the spotting scope to give us a clear view to judge the male. "Got 'em in the scope," he said squinting through the lens. "Take a look. He's broomed on one side."

"He's gotta be thirty-six or seven," I said excitedly. "I can live with the broomed horn but I like how he flares on the long horn."

We played a combination waiting game/stalk as their feeding hour approached that evening. The limits of my balance were tested on the steep climb to our feeding sheep. I moved to within 250 yards, found a good rifle-rest, and dry-fired once to calm my nerves. Cranking in a round, I sighted and fired for real.

"Hit him again!," Tony barked.

"Why?" I returned. "He's dead. Just doesn't know it yet. See the red spot on his shoulder?"

He was dead. Perhaps I was stubborn but I attribute my disobeying orders to my inability to think logically. Tony had seen many more sheep than I taken by hunters. These northern sheep are tough. Many outdoorsman believe it is because of the harsh winters they must endure. While dressing the animal, I noted both that shoulders were broken and the heart destroyed. He was 37 inches on the long horn with a 13 and one-half inch base. We packed him up and headed for camp, where Wade and Hugh had already hung sheep quarters on the meat-pole. Wade had taken a beautiful ram hours before I had taken mine. After that, we concentrated on caribou.

The next day we rode to an area where the guides had found caribou. We rode for two hours until we saw a respectable bull quartering away from us at 400 yards. I wasn't particular about caribou. The Dall sheep was my prize.

"Don't know if I should take him," I pondered. "I don't care about a caribou, anyway,"

"Up to you," replied Tony. "We can always find another."

"If I took him," I said. "I would like to get him mounted in the velvet."

Summertime caribou antlers were covered with a thick, luxurious velvet-like casement that supplied the new antlers with nourishment.

"Oh, take him, Bill," said Tony with a grin.

We stalked to within 225 yards where I supported my seven millimeter in a prone position. The spitzer from my rifle folded the bull, instantly. While Tony dressed the bull, I munched wild blueberries growing at the site.

My fall hunting in Wyoming had proved unsuccessful that year. I was more interested in pursuing another type of game, one that had two legs. After a short courtship, Ricki and I were married the following summer in Cheyenne. She came from a hunting family so my escapades were not unwelcome. Before I met Ricki, I arranged a fall whitetail hunt in Alberta for late November. When I flew to Edmonton, thoughts of my future wife followed me. I hunted whitetail with a fellow named Dallas for a week. The West had just suffered a killer winter in 1983-84 that decimated deer herds. Alberta had already lost a fair number of whitetail bucks just two years prior.

Dallas and his boss, Charlie, had just lost a majority of their whitetail lease when the farmer had second thoughts with the deer population being down. There I was, contending with those factors and I was seriously in love for the first time in my life. Whitetail bucks were supposed to be off guard due to the deer rut but I was the one faltering, entranced by a female.

On my fourth day, Dallas left me to watch a field while he sought permission from another landowner. About one o'clock, I stood and saw a buck running away from me at 200 yards. Throwing up my binoculars for a better look was a mistake; it should have been my rifle. Hell, I could see that big basket with my naked eye. His horns extended past his ears, with tines reaching up almost a foot high. By the time my rifle was up, he had dashed 350 yards and was quartering away, fast. I waited for him to stop but an animal that size doesn't stop near danger. And when he did, 700 yards separated us. He didn't wait three seconds before sliding into the cottonwoods. My indecision foiled me again. Many times, an escaping animal leaves no time for thought. I had never been so indecisive before my accident.

I stood with my jaw dropped. I had stood paralyzed when I should have been shooting at that buck. It was my only chance at filling the deer tag. I returned to Cheyenne with valuable whitetail experience and turned to dear hunting.

After Ricki and I were married we made an unsuccessful move to Jackson Hole and ended up settling in Laramie. I made a fortunate hunt for a young mule deer buck near Laramie, then we traveled across the state for antelope. Because I thought we would be living in Jackson Hole, I drew an antelope area south of there. Ricki and I hunted her Uncle Ed's ranch near Farson, Wyoming. Ricki had hunted pheasants with me the previous year, but this was the first big-game hunt that we would embark on together. She was too compassionate to pull the trigger on an animal but didn't mind if I did. Wade invited me to hunt elk with him and his friend, Terry, on Kennady Peak, west of Laramie.

Kennady is good elk hunting but I had always avoided it due to its popularity. The problem was that the 8000 foot mountain was too accessible from roads. On the other hand, a downed elk on Kennady wasn't difficult to pack out.

When I had bow-hunted the mountain with Wade that September, I learned much of the land. We saw elk within rifle range but didn't even get to notch an arrow. When the October 15th opener came, we had erected a two tents part way up the mountain and were using Wade and Terry's trucks. It was a dry fall with noisy walking conditions. Wade saw elk on opening day but due to the cracking leaves and twigs he couldn't get close enough to them. The story remained the same for the next four days. Terry and Wade had cow tags so they weren't allowed to shoot a bull. They spotted some elk but by the time they could make out the sex, the elk spooked. I hadn't seen any elk, but I had a beautiful four-point mule deer in my sights for fun. With the season closed on mule deer, I waved him along and continued hunting elk.

As we cooked supper that evening, the weather started to change. "Hope this little spell gives us a break," said Terry in his Dutch accent. He was heating beef stew. "Ain't like the fall up here. More like summer."

"We can use any break we can get," said Wade, while drinking a cola. "If I could have just another few seconds on opening day."

When we woke early the next morning, snow was whipping through the air. Planning to hit one drainage that we were familiar with, Wade left Terry and me to hunt it high while he entered lower downstream. I was dressed for the weather but couldn't help shudder from the cold and wind. Terry took one side of the creek and I the other as we crept downward at a snail's pace. I spent three or four times more watching than I did walking.

Elk can betray their presence in thick timber with musky scent. I caught a whiff of elk as snow whirled about me. We knew that inclement weather makes animals uneasy and they feed more. I spied a tan log in front of me that suddenly moved. I froze when I saw no horns on the feeding cow. I used the cover to skirt her, circling uphill, alert for more elk. One elk revealed himself almost straight downhill. When I saw the spikes protruding from his head, my .338 rifle roared seconds behind Terry's .35 Whelen. *Now what are the odds of us both scoring simultaneously?* I thought.

It took the three of us, with the help of another hunter, a few hours to dismember and pack out the two elk. Perhaps it was an inability to follow directions or a touch of envy on Wade's part but the two of us locked horns over the episode. In hindsight, it was a number of things that started our fight including my inability to think clearly and speedily.

"Did you bring my rope," asked Wade.

"Didn't think we'd need it, yet," I answered.

"Can't you follow directions," fumed Wade, throwing his belt-pack on the ground.

The more pressure Wade put on me, the worse my condition became until I couldn't talk to or look at Wade. I spent most of my time visiting with another hunter who camped next to us who was older and more sympathetic. The next day, Wade and Terry continued hunting while I hitched a ride to the nearest telephone. My five-months pregnant wife said she would drive the 50 miles to get me off the mountain. When I returned to camp to wait for my wife, my companions had returned with a cow elk for Wade.

Wade and I almost immediately reconciled, and our falling out became a learning tool for both of us. Wade got a better handle on my limitations and I became more effective at handling stress. Finding a hunting companion had been difficult for me. It's hard to realize the limitaions of someone who isn't visibly impaired.

My impairment followed me to Texas, where I kept looking for a whitetail deer.

Deer have always been high on my trophy list, if not number one. I had always wanted to hunt deer in Texas and with a family on the way, I figured I'd get to it soon. Bitter Creek Trophy Hunts leased a 4400 acre ranch north of San Angelo, Texas where I would try my luck at whitetails and turkey. You could shoot five animals on a Texas deer license, including turkey. I only wanted a trophy since I had plenty of meat in the freezer, but part-owner Randall Adams wanted to control the exploding doe population on the ranch.

I could have tagged does from the word go, but a trophy was on my mind. Stand-hunting was the strategy on my first day, but no trophy crossed my sights. Sitting on a small tower and waiting for the right buck to come along leaves you time to think. Watching the multitude of wildlife on the ranch helped me pass the time. Bobwhite quail, deer and imported goats all roamed the ranch.

Randall and I decided to stretch our legs the second day, opting to walk in an area called Eagle Creek. When we arrived in the area, the hills loomed forlorn but as we advanced, whitetails sprung up everywhere. About an hour into our walk, Randall spotted a nice ten-point buck. I instantly found the deer in my binoculars, not wasting time getting into position. I plopped into a sitting-position as the buck held still. Randall watched the shot.

"You got 'em, Bill," he said in his Texas drawl, "He ain't goin' nowhere. Let's git 'em and git on to a turkey." After dressing him, I dragged the buck to where Randall could get the truck to him. He was nothing to write home about, but plenty good for my first whitetail. By the time we'd finished our walk, I'd taken two does and a tom turkey.

The good time I had in Texas was tempered by the airline losing my whitetail trophy. I had the worst possible thoughts about what had happened to my buck. If I hadn't made a side trip to see my brother and sister-in-law in Houston, the deer probably would have never been lost. At any rate, my whitetail showed up several days after I returned to Cheyenne. Having been adequately salted, the cape was in good shape. We received the processed venison via truck several weeks later. We had plenty of game in the freezer to feed us until the next fall.

My appetite for a large mule deer buck was greateer than any other game trophy, but finding a ranch where they exist is getting to be more difficult everywhere. Packing into remote areas was both complicated and expensive. I was lucky enough to secure permission for deer hunting near Wheatland, Wyoming. I looked forward to the fall.

Roger Schroeder lived less than 50 miles from my house in Laramie. I made the drive the night before I was supposed to hunt and was shown the ranch by one of Roger's ranch hands. We saw a nice 24 inch buck, but I held off, hoping that I would see better the next few days.

Rodger's friend, Mick, hunted with me the next day. We scoured ridges and climbed canyons. Finally, while driving near the western border of the ranch, we spotted a 28-inch, heavy buck bedded down on a hillside where he could watch every approach. I could have taken him at 350 yards but Mick was unsure of my shooting-ability, and wanted to get me closer. We climbed the hill that my buck was laying on from the reverse side. Once over the top, we snuck down on him until we were within forty yards. There was no open shot at first due to the bitterbrush.

We were as stealthy as cats until Mick made a misstep on some loose rock, sending the buck exploding from his bed. He provided a good running shot that I should have taken, but my indecision paralyzed me. As it was, he finally stopped at 600 yards to blow snot at us before disappearing into some rocks. *How many opportunities can I miss on this hunt?* I thought.

When we arrived back at the ranch house, Schroeder told me not to worry about it, that I would get another shot. So off in a different direction we went. We crossed a barren flat that disguised the beautiful canyon beyond. By about 3:30 P.M. we'd arrived in vast, good deer country. Mick and I sat in the vehicle searching the land with binoculars. He found two respectable bucks in the brush. One had high antlers while the other's were extremely flat. I looked over to the left to see a high-horned buck quietly chewing his cud.

"How 'bout this one over here," I said. "'bout twenty-six or seven, you think?"

Mick shook his head. "Don't know if ya can get a closer shot at him than where he's bedded at."

"I'm not pulling another stalk like on that last buck," I replied, shaking my head as well. "I can sneak a little closer but I bet I can hit a three hundred yard shot off that little rim."

We exited the truck slowly, hugging the bitterbrush while looking for a closer shot. Bedded, the buck didn't offer me as large a target as if he were standing up. I had made as long a shot on coyotes without the help of a bipod, which was screwed into my rifle. I extended out the bipod legs slowly and took a firm sitting position behind the rifle. Adjusting my rifle scope to nine-power, I settled on a solid position for the shot. Mick nodded at my thumbs-up sign as I hugged into the supported rifle. I fired.

"You hit 'em," Mick cheered, looking through his binoculars. "He's not going far."

The buck was up and running at the shot but as Mick predicted, he didn't run 20 steps when he fell dead. He was slightly under 27 inches wide but was heavy and symmetrical. He scored within 12 points of the Boone & Crockett record book. I became a deer-guide in 1991.

I helped two Desert Storm veterans score on mule deer in Wyoming. My brother Reuben and his pilot, Tim Schweiger, flew 18 hours during the first day of Desert Storm. The war was the first combat test for the new F-18D Hornet. Their squadron had the only two-seat F-18 in the entire military. During their first week in the theater, I offered them invitations to hunt mule deer in Wyoming that fall. Obtaining a deer license was no problem with Reuben's Wyoming residency. However, the non-resident pilot missed the deer drawing. He had to settle for a license that had not been drawn.

Like an outfitter, I wrote, *No problem. I'll find a place for Tim to hunt here in Southeast Wyoming.* Really there were problems, due to my inability to grasp complex situations. Although I extended hunting invitations regularly, I always felt nervous hosting other hunters. I could find ranches for them to hunt, but I had no experience pursuing deer in these places.

When late October came around after the war, the two fliers relished hunting deer. I found a ranch about 22 miles from my parents home in Cheyenne for Tim—whose squadron named him Onion—to hunt. My deer guide experience before my entry into the service colored my advice throughout the hunt, advice ranging from what to bring to how to sight in their rifles. At times, I realized my advice became overbearing.

We drove to the ranch, west of Cheyenne, early on October 20, 1991. We were greeted by the landowner, who proceeded to prime Tim with tales of big bucks. Reuben wanted Tim to hold out as well and get a good buck. Hands in my pockets, I just rolled my eyes. Deer hunting tales were all the same. As the sun lightened the sky, we planned our strategy. After getting directions from the rancher, we sent Onion up a ridge well before daylight; I liked to hunt deer from the top down. After the lanky Pennsylvanian declined seven does, we put on a drive for the hair-trigger pilot. We separated, with me going high and my little brother hugging the bitterbrush below.

I motioned Tim to join me after I emerged from the pines, and was perplexed when he didn't comply. Little did I know that Reuben had found some bucks and was simultaneously motioning Tim to follow him. Reuben had spooked out a forked-horn while Tim was playing hide and seek with another.

Sneaking up to the lip, Tim finally spotted the male deer almost straight under him. Reuben continued to gesture downwards until Tim shouldered his Remington rifle and fired. It took them some searching among the rocks before they approached the 24 inch mulie. After the traditional handshakes, Reuben hurried to find me. I was busy having coffee with the landowner.

"You gonna help drag?" he said, teasing. "Of course, you can finish your coffee."

I took some ribbing about my qualifications as a mule deer guide, but felt less pressure with one deer tagged. Reuben's buck awaited us north of Cheyenne in Sybille Canyon.

Talk drifted through the day but deer hunting stole the conversation at dinner. When we finished, our truck was readied for Reuben's hunt in Sybille Canyon. The 70 mile drive went quickly and deer started appearing everywhere on our drive in. Tim was climbing out of the cab in excitement.

"Look at that three-point climbing the ridge with his harem." He quickly pointed.

"You'd think he still had a deer-tag left to fill with all that energy," I said as we wound up the mountain.

"He was the same in Kuwait," my brother explained. "Onion's good but excitable."

Peeking over ledges and rims, we spotted numerous does and young bucks. We kept looking but the big deer didn't seem to be in the area. Reuben was anxious to fill his tag and return to El Toro. We four-wheeled back to the rancher's house. The rancher answered the door in his bathrobe, drying his face with a towel. We had pulled him out of the shower.

"We saw some smaller bucks but we're concerned about your four-point buck management policy," Reuben said.

"If you don't want to hold out for a four-point, go ahead and take what you want," the rancher said, water droplets falling from his hair. "After what you guys did in Kuwait, you deserve it."

With that authorization, we proceeded to some ridges that were previously unhunted. When Reuben steered my truck into the area, deer started appearing throughout the hills. Tim was bubbling with excitement once more but I kept a hand on him so he wouldn't exit the truck too soon again.

"Let's go get 'em," clamored the excited pilot.

"You already got your buck," Reuben shot back. "Now it's my turn."

I dropped back, deciding two people were harder to see than three. Tim and Reuben utilized the terrain to get closer to the ridge-hugging deer herd. As they edged closer to the herd, two bucks appeared in a nearby draw.

"They aren't four-points but maybe they'll do," Reuben sighed. "Maybe I better hold out for a better buck."

"Aw, come on, Bone," coerced Tim. "That's over a hundred pounds of good deer jerky."

I was busy erecting a tent when I heard the rifle pop. I thought that I'd better finish erecting the tent, just in case Reuben missed. He hadn't. He wasn't the four-point that we had hoped for but the three-by-two mule deer was reason enough to leave and get back to two wives that spent an eternity without their husbands earlier that year.

When I was visiting with my taxidermist about the hunt, I related that I had a coupon for a whitetail deer hunt near Sheridan, Wyoming. He advised that a northern whitetail mounted next to my Texas buck would be a good comparison of the two types of deer.

I found a companion for the trip. Wade and I teamed up for the hunt, which would take place on U.S. Senator Malcolm Wallop's ranch. The affair was only to be three days, which was probably why the hunt was so reasonable. The Wallop Ranch had a good reputation for big bucks. We would spend Thanksgiving without our families as Wade negotiated the hunt to coincide with the deer rut. We took my truck, but Wade drove. Wade knew I wasn't comfortable in driving long distances due to my impairments. We made good time on the road north.

When we arrived at the ranch, we were greeted by foreman Jim Roach, who gave us a tour of the ranch and then turned us loose. We preferred hunting on our own. On our first day we familiarized ourselves with animal patterns on the ranch. We stand-hunted or walked, depending on the time of day. The second day was more productive as we spotted more bucks. I was stalking a high-horned deer when I heard one shot in the distance. At the same time my approach was ruined by a couple of does I had flushed that ran right into the buck and drove him off. When I caught up with Wade, he was finishing a short drag with a nice nine-point whitetail buck.

"I played cat and mouse with 'em in that brush." He gestured to a thicket. "When he stuck his head out, I took 'em."

"Sun's almost down," I noted. "Hope we have the weather for tomorrow."

We drove the five miles back to the Holiday Inn in Sheridan amid wind and swirling clouds. When we woke the next morning, snow filled the air. A major storm had blown in. Whitetails were everywhere on our drive out to the ranch. We cruised back and forth in the clouds, wondering how we could hunt deer if we couldn't see them. Stand-hunting would have been useless. Depression settled on me as I began to concede defeat.

"Hey, Bill," snapped Wade while driving. "Pull out of it. You're getting me depressed."

"Can't help it," I confessed. "Think the weather has a lot to do with it. How 'bout those whitetails that we saw near the ranch house? Were they on the senator's land?"

We turned back to the house to apply those questions to Roach. When we found that the field was on the ranch, we made a bee line in that direction. The deer were where we had spotted them previously, with two nice bucks dominating the group. We watched from 700 yards as hormones made the bucks oblivious to our presence. There was no cover for a stalk on these deer save the storm and their preoccupation with the rut. Duckwalking was our choice of maneuver on the preoccupied herd.

Two hundred yards lay between us and our quarry. When the deer looked our way, we froze. I set up my bipod and ducked into a sitting position. With the snow, I had a hard time keeping track of the heavy-horned buck I wanted to claim.

"Which one is he, Wade?" I whispered. "They keep moving around."

"The one by the fence post," he said, ice ringing his mustached mouth. "I know, this snow makes it tough."

"Okay; this is it," I warned.

I fired.

"Hit 'em again," Wade ordered.

I couldn't believe that the deer still stood. I shoved the rifle at Wade.

"Here," I commanded. "You shoot 'em."

Wade half-heartedly accepted the rifle, but before he could shoot, the buck fell. We ran to the buck and I punched my deer-tag, dressed him, and sat shivering more from the excitement than from the cold. This whitetail was the heaviest-horned ever taken off the Wallop Ranch in Jim Roach's memory. With my Wyoming buck alongside the Texas whitetail, no one could doubt which state had bigger deer.

Wally Needham, of Cheyenne, always led a week-long foray to Grand Teton National Park for the annual depredation hunt in early November. Wally had invited me along years earlier. I had just had minor foot surgery, and was looking for an easy hunt, so I accepted. When fall snows envelop northwest Wyoming, the Grand Teton and Yellowstone elk herds make for the National Elk Refuge near Jackson Hole. The trick was to intercept elk between their summer home and the feedground. If we were in the right place, elk would practically run right over us to get by. I chose to hunt the hayfields because the area was easy to negotiate. Blacktail Butte and the river bottoms were the other choices, but were more physically demanding. We were blessed with snowfall almost all week, but it was dry our first day in Jackson Hole so the elk hunting was pretty spotty.

On the third day in Jackson, the weather changed. My hunting partner, Fred David, and I watched the Teton herd across the Snake, in the safety of a no-shooting zone. They were edging their way toward the elk refuge but they knew the danger that lay between them and the feedground. They continued looking toward the refuge but made no move until dark. We returned to our apartment in Jackson where we could trade information.

"Boy, you could see them wanting to come across but they were holding back," I said as Fred drove.

"Don't tell the guys anything we saw until we find out what information they have," whispered David, as if our crew was listening in. "We'll plan a strategy for all six of us."

A Cheyenne game warden was part of our crew, and he enlisted a local officer to brief us on the elk situation in Jackson. We all huddled around Bill as he told all in the motel.

"They're coming across tonight, fellas," said the young warden. "The river bottoms, hayfields, and Blacktail should all be good in the morning."

I looked at Fred. "Guess our secret is out."

"Oh, you two were gonna withhold information?" said Wally, grinning.

"No, Bill just beat us to the story," I answered. "We were going to tell and get our heads together for a morning hunt."

The next morning, Fred and I drove to the east of the hayfields, advancing along a set of telephone poles.

"Let's hunker on this ditch," said Fred. "They can come from anywhere so we better get a place where we're safe from gunfire."

With the rising sun at our backs, we could hear shots just north of us. Then out of a line of trees to our front, two elk cows appeared. Bill had told us the night before that he would like us to kill cows so as to reduce the Grand Teton herd. There were orange garments all around us, betraying hunters who were busy spitting bullets at the pair. I rose on one knee and fired after Fred did. Slipping back into the ditch, we took cover while the lead flew. I didn't like this. But David and I hurried to find a blood trail after the shooting quit.

"I don't think I hit her," Fred admitted, walking quickly. "That was some barrage everyone fired back there."

"Yeah, that gunfire had me more worried about getting hit than dropping an elk," I agreed. "All those bullets flying is why the Game and Fish requires everyone to have certified safety instruction. I still don't know if I like all that shooting."

We found both elk being dressed out by the hunters who had claimed them. Elk hunting is often just a morning hunt up there so we finished the day by making a run up to Yellowstone National Park, just for fun. Unless the elk are moving, you might as well stay home. But when they are, your chances of filling an elk tag are pretty good. On our fifth day, we were prompted to try the south end of the hayfields where Steve and and his friend Keith werre concentrating. As we drove to a parking area, we could see tan silhouettes in the field before us.

"Five cows," Fred said, excitedly. "I'll go along this fence while you see if that ditch can get you close enough for a shot."

The cows were obviously confused by being caught out in the open. I slithered down the trench as David fired on one elk. The cow drropped. I stalked as far as I could down the ditch, edging out as the quartet danced before me at 200 yards. Plopping into a sitting position, I cut loose with my .338 as well. Some say that .338 is too much rifle for elk and it was in this case. The cow I aimed at kept walking while the one behind her fell dead with a broken neck.

I scratched my head and stood up just as the elk I was shooting at fell dead as well. This made me very nervous. I had two elk down in Grand Teton National Park. Riding up on a horse, a park official said that he saw the whole episode. He asked if I would like for him to find someone to tag the additional elk. I quickly agreed. An older man from Buffalo, Wyoming pulled his sled toward the kill site.

"That ranger asked if someone wanted to tag an elk," he said as he trudged up to the kill. "I said I bet that fella's awful nervous with two elk down in the national park."

We quickly proceeded to dress both animals in the snowy morning. That was my introduction to depredation elk hunting at Jackson Hole. And although having an elk come to me was neat, I'd much rather hunt them.

Camouflaged to the teeth, the author hunts black bear with his muzzle-loader near Gunnison, Colorado in 1982.

Padilla harvested this gobbler in South Dakota in 1984. He located the bird by hooting like an owl.

Wade Dumont holds two whitetail bucks he and the author took on U.S. Senator Malcolm Wallop's ranch near Sheridan, Wyoming.

Northwest Territories quartet celebrate after a successful Canadian sheep/caribou hunt in 1986. From left: Wade Dumont, the author, Wally Needham and Joel Schaefer.

Padilla added a Texas whitetail to his collection in 1988. He hunted near Sweetwater, Texas in early December.

Rio Grande turkey were a bonus on a Texas whitetail hunt in December 1988.

The author calls to tom turkey near Lusk, Wyoming in 1989.

Padilla adds another turkey to the freezer near Lusk, Wyoming in 1989.

Padilla surveys the Canadian Wilderness during his sheep/caribou hunt in 1996.

Padilla scouts "The Devil's Armchair" for bighorn sheep during his 1986 Colorado hunt. This was a hunt where Padilla was not successful.

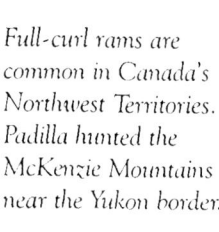
Full-curl rams are common in Canada's Northwest Territories. Padilla hunted the McKenzie Mountains near the Yukon border.

Ricki Padilla, the author's wife, hams it up with their pet Malamute in Laramie, Wyoming. Bill and Ricki moved to Laramie after they were married in 1987.

Marine aviator Tim Schweiger and the author's brother were guided by Padilla to mule deer after the two officers fought in Kuwait during Desert Storm in 1991.

The author made a three-hundred-yard shot on this fine mule deer buck near Wheatland, Wyoming.

Breaking in the pup on blue-grouse, the author and Chesapeake Bay Retriever, Cookie, grin over a successful hunt.

Another hunter in the wings. Padilla's firstborn, Antonio, at two years old.

The author with a fine Wyoming antelope he harvested late in the season during 1991.

Chapter 12
Bad Luck Bulls

Foul-smelling, dank, bear breath woke Wyoming elk guide Gary Capron while I dreamed of Wind River Mountain bulls.

"Bill, Bill," he whispered excitedly. "Get your gun."

I woke to glimpse the bear swapping ends, heading for the nearby timber after exiting our tent. We staked the corner of the wall-tent the next morning.

Wyoming and the entire West suffered a severe drought the summer of '94. Fires erupted everywhere in the West, and Big Sandy in Wyoming's Wind River Mountains was not immune. Smoke and ash permeated the air in Black Joe drainage from a fire north of Pinedale, Wyoming. This drought had retarded the berry crop that sustained black bears.

Nearly every western state had their share of bear problems as the critters sought to replace their food source. I was hoping to take a fine bull elk from outfitter and old friend Bob Lowe's limited quota elk zone.

My marriage, young family and disability had curtailed my archery for nearly ten years. I wanted to experience the thrill of doing it again.

My desire to hunt effectively again drove me through the deficient concentration, coordination and balance difficulties, faulty logic and other associated disabilities.

Lowe was anxious to have a bowhunter in his Big Sandy Camp. Arrowhead Outfitter's camp had never been hunted by archers, though Lowe maintains a high success ratio on elk. Many years, he will achieve 100 percent success on elk. I had a bear license in my pocket, just in case we should encounter a camp-raider.

We heard a black bear in our tent my first night in camp. While coursing the area, we heard more bears in the aspen throughout the ride.

Gary heard elk in the timber but they did not respond to our calls. I wondered if I had booked this hunt too early in September. Bob Lowe rode into camp my third day, quickly issuing me a rain check for later in the month when the elk would probably respond better.

When I returned later that month, Wyoming clouds were trying to compensate for the dry summer. I was nursing a sore finger that had required stitches when I negligently attempted to change broadheads without a broadhead wrench.

Capron took me to a place where we had found elk two weeks prior. The young ex-Marine couldn't get elk to answer due to the rain. After the clouds opened up later in the day, we heard an elk blast that shook our saddles.

We tied our horses, quickly preparing to coax the beast within range. I sprayed elk urine on us and prepared myself. After nearly an hour of cow-talk and bugles, the young guide access the situation.

"I wonder if he saw our horses?"

"We should go after him," I advised.

Capron was eager, outpacing me in our dash across the stream-bed, onto the upward sloping spruce. We glanced back to see the horses tethered in plain sight for the bull to see. I hoped that our error hadn't frightened the bull completely.

About 40 yards into the timber, Gary invited the bull again with his Eastman Cow-Call. Darkness was approaching. I heard cows mewing uphill, to my right.

Gary emitted a shrill group of notes that challenged the bull. Within minutes, I saw his legs in the trees at 50 yards ahead and to my right. He turned, displaying his ivory-tided, six-by-six rack, finally quartering away from me at 30 yards.

I drew my PSE Laser Magnum with confidence, which eroded when my peep-sight didn't align.

"Damn," I quietly mouthed.

Frantically trying to turn the peep with my fingers wasn't cutting it. I decided to redraw, and my arrow clinked off the arrowrest. The bull's rear and legs stiffened at the sound. He dug for safer ground in the timber.

Sighing, I was relieved when the elk returned to Gary's cow-talk invitation. Eventually, darkness surrounded us and I returned to Gary's perch.

"You screwed up, didn't you?" chastised the wiry guide, jokingly.

"My peep wouldn't align."

Gary shrugged. "He would have come closer."

We returned to camp, making the ambush site a staging area for the next day. Between my failure with that bull and worrying over a home construction difficulty, I didn't sleep much that night. Sleep had been intermittent for me the past 14 years. Chemical changes in my brain had affected my sleep patterns.

I decided to snooze the following morning. There was no use forcing the hunt while I was exhausted. Capron and I traded horses for mules that day, me carrying my bow in hand while I rode.

We took a short break to go fishing at mid-day, then pressed on. My mule thought that she had enough of my waving the bow from arm to arm, over her head. The big female bolted at high speed as I tried to rein her in with my partially paralyzed left arm.

It was no use, so I bailed out recalling a cousin who had been dragged by a mule to his death. Gary quickly rushed to my aid.

"We're on an elk hunt, huh?" I said, confusedly.

"Yeah, that fall made your bell ring," he said, supporting me.

"It doesn't take much to make my bell ring," I explained. "Doctors have explained that once you've had a head-injury, you can be more susceptible to one."

I picked up my bow, disgusted. The cams of the compound bow were uneven after the fall. My sights hung from a broken brass screw. My bowhunt was ended, but my .338 Mauser Mark-X was in camp, awaiting the rifle season in two days. I had learned to be flexible throughout my recovery.

Bob Lowe arrived after succesfully finishing a bighorn-sheep hunt. Gary and I met the new party at the Big Sandy Creek trailhead and made the ride into his Big Sandy Camp together.

We separated, three hunters to each guide for the next day. University of Michigan researcher Steve Heeringa and ex-college quarterback Dave Wood would accompany Bob and I to hunt the timberline where elk had been driven by heat and domestic sheep. Snowflakes permeated the air now, promising to create better hunting conditions at the 9500 feet elevation. Domestic sheep had been removed from the area on September 15th.

We fixed our optics on several bulls above the timberline on our ride upward. One good six-by-six bull resided on the ridgeline to our right.

The stocky, blond outfitter left Steve and I in a swirling blizzard as he took Dave after the big stag. Steve and I positioned ourselves to cover the ridge with gunfire should any elk return. Elk tracks littered the hillside. Lowe had allowed me to extend my hunt a few days but I had a Veteran's Administration appointment approaching. I wasn't going to be too selective.

When the pair returned after three hours, they reported that their quarry had moved. We chose to cross the steep, snowy basin in search of of the two smaller bulls we saw resting on the adjacent ridge.

As we traversed the bowl that separated us from our objectives, I spent as much time on my rump as on my feet. At first I blamed my footwear but then I noticed that the outfitter was wearing the same tread-pattern on his boots. Falling into the trap of blaming my head injury for my frequent slipping, I cursed myself for booking the hunt. I continued after the bulls like a drunken fool until Bob witnessed my dilemma and offered to carry my rifle.

"Sure, Bwana," I sighed, reliquishing my .338.

I felt silly by having someone carry my firearm, but I knew that my limitaions required it. The other two hunters were not falling like I was.

I retieved my rifle when walking became less treacherous. As we approached the ridge, I smelled that "barnyard" elk scent prevalent to concentrations of elk. One five-by-four bull and two cows exploded from their beds on the reverse side of the uplift. I shouldered my .338 quickly and I found the bull's neck in my sight at 80 yards. I only had two rounds with me. I used one for the knockdown and the other for a quick coup-de-grace when I overtook the fallen bull.

Packing plenty of elk meat for my freezer help relieve the depression I had suffered over the six-by-six bull that escaped my bow days earlier.

I'll be back someday, I told myself as I dressed my elk. With a self-aligning peep-sight for my bow.

One of the reasons I chose to hunt elk in Big Sandy was that I had a goose-hunt scheduled for mid-October, when I normally hunt elk. Wade and I both had supported the Rocky Mountain Elk Foundation for years. The bird hunt was being auctioned off at their annual Cheyenne banquet. When Wade and I bid $100 for a two-day goose hunt in North Dakota, we expected to get raised quickly.

Perhaps no other hunter was game enough to drive 600 miles for a two-day hunt. Or maybe everyone knew something that we didn't.

When the day finally arrived in late October, some local storms had blown the majority of the geese south toward the gulfcoast. Our host was a liquor-distributor from Grand Forks, North Dakota. "Cash" Register felt so bad about our dilemma, he invited us to try again the following year.

Wade balked but I was quick to accept Cash's suggestion. Geese are attracted to northeast North Dakota by the bountiful grain crops there while on their way south to Arkansas and Texas. The difficulty with hunting waterfowl in North Dakota is that the window of opportunity is short. I flew to Grand Forks via Denver, Colorado in mid-October, 1994. Cash greeted me at the small airport with bad news for the second straight year.

"Are the geese in this year, Cash?" I asked enthusiastically. "The weather has been awful warm this fall."

"That's just it, Bill," he replied. "The weather has been so warm this year that there are damn few geese around."

"Just my luck," I lamented. "Wade was afraid of this happening."

Driving the 100 miles to Edgland, we saw lots of ducks in the adjacent potholes along the highway. But I had flown here to hunt geese. We put out decoys the following morning at nearby Snider Lake. We climbed into rockpiles and called at snow and blue geese.

Naturally, the few geese on the lake went in the opposite direction. We were left to try different tactics for the remainder of the morning. At least there were geese around. Cash had painted a dreary picture of the hunting for me so that anything better would seem like gravy.

"Let's pick up and drive," ordered Cash, who knew of more areas to find geese.

North Dakota allows hunters to enter private property unless that land is posted against trespassing. That being the case, we cruised the checkerboard of farm roads, looking for birds on the ground. We would sneak as close as we dared, shooting at loners or groups of honkers as they frequented the main flock on the property.

There must have been hundreds of geese atop a little knoll, south of the road. We debarked Cash's Suburban, beelining for a high stand of brush at the foot of the hill. Cash covered one end of the rise and I covered another. Having no call, I relied on Cash to bring geese our way. We both were shooting 3 inch twelve-guages.

The main flock was far enough away so that our shooting at lone geese didn't disturb the bunch, initially. Pass-shooting, without decoys, has never been my favorite way of hunting geese. Decoys bring the geese close enough so a gunner can target the head and neck. Pass-shooting usually yields longer shots, making the required steel shot not as effective.

Shooting simultaneously, we could hear the inferior steel hitting our targets, but the geese flew on. We watched the birds, hoping the wounded geese would fall from the formation. One group came directly over my head.

Twenty-five yards is more like the distance I was accustomed to shooting from. A gorgeous blue winged by, and I swung to follow him with my Remington 11-87. I targeted his neck, fired and watched the plummeting target.

"Good shot, Bill!" Cash shouted. "No doubt about that bird."

We tracked down two more snows that had been taken down by our barrage. Cash steered the four-by-four toward more geese we saw punctuating the horizon. Other hunters were using the same strategy, outmaneuvering us to several flocks.

Several times, Cash dumped me out to shoot at birds while we steered for the opposite side of the feeding swarm. Since North Dakota only allows goose hunting in the morning, our first day ended rather quickly.

"That first morning wasn't as bad as you led me to expect," I admonished Cash while strapping into the vehicle.

"No," he said, grinning. "After last year, I had to be sure that you wouldn't be disappointed. These geese are just the vanguard of the big flocks, still up in Manitoba."

We rested, cleaned up, and prepared in anticipation of the following crisp morning. We knew from our scouting drive that afternoon where to ambush birds close to Edgland. Problem was that every hunter in the locale knew about those geese too.

When we converged on those birds, experience told Cash to anticipate the flock's escape-route from the other waterfowlers. Watching the wind, posted terrain, and the other hunters, we steered for a set of ditches that would conceal us.

Cash ejected me from the four-by-four while he removed the vehicle from the scene. I had unloaded my weapon while in the black Chevrolet. Hopping into a ditch, I brought my firearm to bear on the first bunch of birds over my head.

I placed the shotgun-bead on an elegant blue sailing overhead at 20 yards, aimed and pulled the trigger.

My gun was empty. Geese were enveloping me while I fumbled for non-existent shells in my camouflage coat. All my shells were sitting on the floor of Cash's Suburban.

One befuddled liquor wholesaler watched me through his compact optics, a smile on his weathered face. Birds were practically knocking me off my feet while I stared at Cash, a disgusted expression on my face. Cash collected me after every goose had safely escaped. We sped to nearby Agate, "The Goose Capitol of North Dakota."

"Look over on the right," I blurted. "They're everywhere!"

"I know a spot we can work that flock from," he said.

Ditching our vehicle, we eased into a pair of barrow pits near the road. It was easy to sneak our way toward the geese. Cash issued instruction when we parted company.

"There's two flocks out there. If we can get between them, there's sure to be some shootin'."

Water stood in the ditch I chose for cover. I did my best to stay dry when I spied a black cloud coming my way.

Hot damn, I thought. *Here they come.*

I steadied myself on a steep bank, following a group of geese with my gun. They came closer, closer, until my shotgun was pointing straight up.

I fired.

Tumbling backward, head over heels, I came to rest in two feet of stagnant, slimy, rainwater in the channel's bottom. A dead snow goose tumbling into the water beside me. Retrieving the goose, mud dripping from my soaked coat, I proceeded to Cash's Suburban.

"McManus would have a field day writing about you," he teased, referring to the humorous outdoor writer. "What a way to end a goose hunt."

Cash drove me back to Grand Forks that afternoon where I swore that I'd be back. Goose hunting is often a weather-determined adventure, anywhere you hunt them. North Dakota can be very good, if you hit the migration.

I began to find bird hunting more fun that big game. Missing was as much fun as dropping your game. It was a lot safer as well for someone like me, who had been through the grind.

Chapter 13
Bighorns

I thought that my 1994 elk hunt would be my last guided big-game hunt. Applying for Wyoming bighorn sheep and moose permits for years with no success had resigned me to the fact. But I began 1995 by drawing one of the most demanded moose areas in the state.

When I had hunted Wyoming moose before, shortly after my injury, I narrowly filled the permit with a small bull on the last day of the hunt. Bob Lowe was tickled to receive my call that April. Though I had hunted with his outfit the previous year, we didn't hunt together but one day. This time it would just be me and Bob, in Grey's River, just like old times.

Bob suggested booking the hunt for later in the season, when snow would drive moose to lower elevations. Grey's River would also have less hunting pressure. I traveled to Jackson Hole on October 22, eight days after the elk season had begun and nearly three weeks into the moose season.

Snow began falling heavily in Jackson when I arrived at the outfitter's home. We drove for Grey's River the next morning arriving at Little Grey's, a tributary of Grey's River, in time to erect camp and hunt the evening. It wasn't long before we found a 30 inch bull in a clearing above camp. Bob set up a spotting scope and quickly offered me a look.

"Naw," I said. "Too early in the hunt to take a mediocre bull."

He agreed, and we continued to hunt. Up we rode, into a herd of elk at the head of the drainage. There weren't any superior bulls to make us quit moose hunting, so we continued the search until evening fell upon us with the western sky painted crimson by the descending sun. We returned to camp.

Upon rising the next day we climbed a ridge, one mile south. By then, six inches of new snow covered the hills, giving us a huge advantage. It wasn't long before we found a new trail of moose track through the spruce. I had never had much luck with long-trailing stalks, but this sign was fresh.

When we emerged onto a small basin, two bull moose greeted us across the basin at 250 yards. The larger bull was 35 inches wide I estimated through my binoculars.

I hastily dismounted, found a log and pointed my .338 Winchester at the moose.

The fiberglass-stocked magnum cracked. The bullet broke the animal's shoulder, sending him tumbling into the bowl. We quickly photographed and dressed the kill, giving us the remainder of the day to pack the animal to camp.

Now we could turn our attention to elk. Seemed like the elk hunters in The Grey's were all near the road. Our horses were a blessing we would quickly put to our advantage.

The third day of the hunt, we began climbing the famous Grayback Ridge of the range. Decades earlier, the Boone & Crockett number two mule deer was taken on the steep divide. On the way up the rise, Bob spotted a small elk herd straddling on a finger ambling east. After minutes of scrutiny, we determined there were no bulls in the group.

Up we rode until Bob glanced over his shoulder, bailing off his mount while reaching for his glasses. I was swift to follow discerning a large bull elk in a small, snow-covered clearing across a canyon. It was big, a six-point at least. But there was no way to stalk closer.

Since this was a guided moose-hunt, we were both hunting elk for ourselves. Bob had dibs on the bull since he had spotted the beast. But we argued for right to the shot.

"I'm gonna take him from here," announced Bob, settling in for the shot.

"With a little .280 Remington?" I countered. "You might tickle him at this range. If we could get closer than 500 yards you should take it. But my rifle is made for a shot like that."

Bob had seen wounded elk before, and this beast was too good a trophy to risk a shot with a .280.

"Guess you're right," he admitted. "But I'm gonna be right behind you with my rifle. That elk isn't gonna escape."

I had already hunkered behind my .338, using a rock and my coat for a rest. The bull stood broadside with the white background giving me an excellent target.

When my .338 sounded, the bull dropped immediately, sliding down into the trees. The bullet had done its job.

"Now you have the rest of the year to hunt elk up here," I proclaimed. "The elk season is almost over in my neck of the woods."

The 500 yard shot ended my three-day moose hunt in Grey's River. The monster turned out to be a seven-by-six bull when we finally picked our way to him. I was thrilled to have taken the pair of trophy animals with no mishap. Perhaps my disability would no longer frustrate my hunting adventures.

The next year I finally drew a Wyoming bighorn sheep permit, after 19 years of applying. I didn't think I would be hunting with Bob again so soon.

Wyoming's bighorn sheep area number four had received much adverse publicity from the Game & Fish in recent years. Pneumonia supposedly had taken a toll on rams in the region. Bob differed with G&F officials though, and convinced me to apply for the sector. I booked the first hunt with Bob that year and carried my bow along to try arrowing a sheep. It wasn't long before I was scrambling through the moutains again.

We had packed 20 miles into the Washakie Wilderness, north of Dubois, Wyoming. After establishing base camp, Bob and I spent days trying to get close enough to a sheep for an arrow.

My Vibram-soled boots kept slipping while I frantically crossed the granite slide. After falling once, I continued across the treacherous slope in guest of a full-curl ram. My feet went out from under me again.

I looked desperately at Bob to the other side. He had crossed without a mishap. My confidence was clouded with doubts in my ability to negotiate the terrain that shielded my Wyoming bighorn sheep. I questioned my sanity to attempt hunting moutain sheep and thought back to my hospitalization at Fitzsimons Army Medical Center in Denver where doctors had told my father that I would never hunt again.

Acquaintances on that neurosurgery ward counseled me through my situation.

"I'm gonna hunt, ride and shoot again, Sergeant Hoffman," I croaked out to the back-injury impaired staff sergeant while walking to physical therapy. "It's too important to me just to quit."

"You can do anything that you want to." Hoffman grimaced, holding his back. "When you quit, you're dead."

"I'm gonna get the Grand Slam," I continued. "That's always been my dream."

Sergeant Charles Hoffman looked uncovinced, smiling weakly but replied, "If you shoot high, you'll hit somewhere in that neighborhood."

In a service medical enviroment, most patients lend encouragement. That "can-do" attitude is prevalent in the military. But I could read the NCO's eyes. He had his doubts.

Many avid hunters know that sheep hunting is one of the most demanding forms of the sport. Sheep hunting isn't for the fair-hearted, weak or feeble, much less the seriously impaired. I knew that I had a long road ahead of me and was anxious to negotiate it.

In the past ten years I had married, fathered two beautiful children and writhed violently in my struggles with recovery. I clung to my illusion of the Grand Slam through it all.

Another guide and a cook accompanied Bob and me into the wilderness in late August. We had a full day's ride ahead of us to reach Gentian Creek, our spike camp.

It was gorgeous country, Wyoming. Though it was my first trip into the Washkie, I related it to other memories I harbor of my home state.

Bob planned to hunt with me four days with a bow and the remaining six days with my 7mm Magnum.

We all saddled the next day and headed for Red Tops. It was an appropriate name for the buttes. Crimson spires dotted the elevation. Bob spotted a half curl ram on our way up. I had doubts about my equilibrium in that high terrain. Questions concerning my wits clouded me as I used my bow for balance like a tightrope walker. We spotted five rams later that afternoon. The two biggest were three-quarter curls but they were feeding on a bench and were unapproachable. Bob devised a strategy to drive the rams by me, which bombed when they scampered by at 60 yards, not close enough for a bow. We turned our efforts to the north side of the peaks where guide Steve Bonomo found seven keepers, over 1000 yards off. Three of the rams approached full-curl. It was too late in the day to contemplate a stalk, but we found a starting point for the following day.

As I was to learn, bighorns move around a lot, at least they did in these mountains. We saw fewer than the 67 sheep we found on our first day. Our third was more productive.

Ross Myers, our cook, left for the trailhead and Dubois to lead another sheep hunter into the drainage. When Bob glassed him riding errantly while we were hunting, he rode swiftly to redirect the cook. Steve and I were left to hunt that afternoon.

We had just ridden into camp when the wiry guide found rams on a butte across the drainage.

"If we hurry, we can be there long before dark," said Bonomo.

About 1500 yards separated us from our prey. We rode hard, putting on a stalk that took us across 60-degree talus slopes. I must have looked like a tightrope walker, using my bow for the pole. But we eased into position, hardly disturbing the dozing quartet of male sheep. The largest was three-quarter curl, 40 yards away.

I drew an Easton Gamegetter, slowly rising to index the sheep below. These sheep didn't even know we were there. Perfect, save for the wind, which blasted us atop that mountain.

At full draw, I couldn't steady the bow enough for a shot and slowly declined. I just couldn't justify such a shot even if the ram was bedded broadside. A ram is too precious for a shot like that to be loosed. After several minutes, the band spotted us above, stared in disbelief and bolted for escape cover.

The next few days were entertaining as we viewed developed male sheep, usually at long distances. My aforementioned balance problem resulted in a full-curl ram losing us in the demanding topography on the fourth day.

I blew my first real chance on day five, after I traded bow for my rifle. Bob Lowe stepped off his mule at mid-morning to glass a basin below us. I followed, binoculars in hand. Bob Coons, an experienced sheep hunter from Houston, paired up with Steve, so Bob and I were on our own. After 10 minutes of looking Bob whirled, an ecstatic expression frozen on his face. He pointed downward. Two mature sheep stared at us, 150 yards away.

I had left my rifle on my mule, forty yards away.

When I dashed for the rifle, the two sheep strode into the basin to find me. I never saw the full-curl and three-quarter explode out of the dish. We returned to camp.

After hunting all morning on my seventh day, I observed through my 8x30 Swarovski's a pretty, chocolate three-quarter curl ram across the canyon on Lost Ranger Top Peak. It was three P.M. when I implored Bob into making the rough, five-mile ride over to him. Steve and Bob Coons would spot from our perch, keeping surveillance.

We blew off the mountain, passed through camp, traded horses for mules and climbed Lost Ranger Top. A 70-degree slope greeted us, protecting the chocolate ram. Bonomo frantically waved his hat, signalling we were just above the quarry, but the climb was impossible. We gathered the mules and left for camp.

On our way across Saddle Creek, Bob pulled out his spotting scope to survey Hard Luck Mountain, behind the camp. He strained his eyes.

"There's two rams up in a basin behind camp," he exclaimed. "One's three-quarter curl."

"It's seven o'clock, Bob," I said. "Let's ride."

Bob and I could get there in an hour without pushing our mounts to the limit. Riding as hard as we dared, we tethered at the lower edge of the basin. Picking through the scattered jack pines, we closed the distance to 300 yards, where we sighted the rams, who were undisturbed.

"I'll shoot from here," I whispered, gripping the fiberglass-stocked rifle.

Finding a fallen log, I settled behind the 3x9 Leupold and brought the rifle to bear. I was rushing the shot needlessly. The round went over the ran's back.

Confused, the sheep sought cover in some rocks, but he was still exposed to me. I breathed deeply and sent another bullet at him.

I would hear the impacting bullet, but he still stood. My third shot broke the ram's shoulder, sending him hurtling down the slide he was climbing.

We admired the ram in the twilight, dressed him and reserved the pack-out and pictures for the following day. He was three-quarter curl, perhaps signifying I was three-quarters of the way to my Grand Slam.

I'm only 42 years old and there's one more ram for me to hunt. I've applied in most desert bighorn states, but if I never draw, I've already proven much to myself and, in my mind, Sergeant Hoffman back in Denver. One day, I'll find that ram.

A brace of snow geese is a good reason to hunt Texas' Gulf Coast. Padilla hunted near Katy, Texas in 1992.

Padilla grins over his hard-won 5-4 bull elk taken in 1994 in Wyoming's Bridger Wilderness.

Sighting down his rifle, Padilla prepares to take the longest shot in his life—five-hundred yards—at a bull elk.

After making the longest shot he has ever attempted, the author proudly holds his 1995 Wyoming bull elk.

Padilla glasses the distance to his bull moose he took in Wyoming's Grey's River in 1995.

Five-hundred yards across—whew! thinks the author as he surveys the distance he shot his seven-by-six Grey's River bull elk.

Padilla sits atop his hard-won, Wyoming Bighorn Sheep he collected in 1996. After trying to score with a bow, Padilla settled for his rifle.

Padilla sits behind his Wyoming bull moose he clobbered in 1995 in that state's Grey's River.

Arrowhead Outfitter's Bob Lowe readies to pack-out Padilla's 35" Shira's Mosse. Padilla connected on the moose on day two of his hunt.

Chapter 14
There is Help

What made these individuals able to fight off the ramifications of their health problems? The answer lies in their will and determination to attempt their sport. They had strong people behind them in their families, friends, and spouses. They saw crutches available to them and anyone suffering from disabilities or health problems. There are organizations, special hunts, and people who are more than willing to lend a helping hand. Let me start with my home state of Wyoming, and list some of the help available to these distinctive people.

Wyoming

Wyoming's Game and Fish Department offers special permits for the mobility-disabled to hunt and shoot from a vehicle. The practice is illegal in Wyoming unless a hunter obtains one of these permits. Many antelope sectors are prime candidates for the vehicle hunter. With the right permit, antelope are the perfect game for someone who can't walk or otherwise get around to hunt. There are some deer areas that can be hunted in the same fashion. Granted, many of these places are on private land, but landowners are usually more receptive to allowing an impaired hunter chase his game. Elk are more difficult to hunt from a vehicle, but as I have written, areas exist in Wyoming where elk can be accessed by the disabled. Pat Clark has had tremendous success with elk near Jackson Hole.

Even the most strenuous of hunts can be accessed by the handicapped. Ken Hall, Roy Kern, and Kirk Atter of Buffalo, Wyoming all have successfully harvested bighorn sheep in Wyoming.

It can be done! Hunters near Douglas, Wyoming have put together a "Helluva Hunt" for disabled hunters in pursuit of antelope. Helluva Hunt has been ongoing since 1985 when outdoor writer Jim Zumbo and Bill Brown first visualized it. Zumbo received a letter from a disgruntled hunter who was battling a disability. He sent the letter to Brown and outfitter Gary Stearns, who first assembled the hunt. Stearns is no longer a professional outfitter, opting to work for the telephone company instead. Thirty volunteer guides and Stearns take the first week of October to stage a Helluva Hunt for disabled hunters. The entire town of Douglas assists.

Rooms are donated by the Holiday Inn, trap-shooting is also available, along with several other services like meat-processing, meals, etc., donated for the hunters.

Helluva Hunt takes place on about 30,000 acres on four different ranches in antelope area #29. Visually-impaired hunters are even encouraged to participate, with special rifles and scopes equipped to help them get their game. These sights are actually two rifle scopes attached to .243 Winchester rifles. The guide can use one scope to assist his hunter zero in on the target. The guide does his best to talk the hunter into a terminal shot on an antelope. Helluva Hunt has transformed into a non-profit organization that attracts hunters from all over the country.

When the hunt began in 1985, mostly local impaired hunters participated but now nearly half of the antelope hunters are from out of state. About 15 hunters are guided by over 25-guides and support personnel to their quarry each year. Helluva Hunt has spread to several states, including Minnesota and Florida. Georgia has a similar hunt of their own conception. Outfitters often cater or will adapt for people struggling through a disadvantage.

Steve Sheaffer of Arlington is the only Wyoming outfitter that advertises for disabled hunters. The burly outdoorsman spends several hundred dollars a year advertising for clients with disabilities. He admits that he has never had a disabled client, though he has dealt with his brother Greg's disability all his life.

Greg has hobbled with cerebral palsy his entire life, and Steve became comfortable in assisting him enjoy the outdoors. Steve also says that he has spoken to many potential clients that have a disability but none ever booked a hunt with him. Disabled people usually lack the confidence that an outfitter can really help them to get their game. Sheaffer has done it for his brother Greg but somehow that confidence can't be conveyed to a stranger. Just about every outfitter that I have spoken with has dealt with hunters who have had heart problems, couldn't walk, or were elderly, except outfitters who specialize in remote, wilderness hunting that requires much horseback riding.

Dale Critchfield of Table Mountain Outfitters in Cheyenne has several hunting spots that would be perfect for most people, regardless of disability. Dale stresses that it is important for the outfitter to know what problems a hunter possesses before the hunt.

"A lot of hunters feel macho and don't want to say that they have a bad heart or can't walk," he told me. "I'd rather have a hunter that has heart problems and tells me, than one that gets us both in trouble on a strenuous hunt."

He goes on to say that some outfitters are concerned about the liability aspects. If an outfitter doesn't want to mess with it, he'll tell you, but many will shoulder the responsibility for an impaired hunter. After all a dollar is a dollar, as Critchfield would say. He also states that an antelope hunt is tailor-made for an impaired hunter. With a little scouting, Critchfield or most outfitters will be able to sit a customer on a waterhole or other natural crossing and in a matter of time, they will be successful. The experienced outfitter would have little problem with anyone on an antelope hunt.

Critchfield once had a buffalo hunter that needed nitroglycerin for his heart at the 6300 foot elevation of Cheyenne. Dale couldn't let the hunter exert himself too much, so he did a bit of scouting and found a waterhole for the hunter to sit on. Getting his buffalo was no trouble.

Other outfitters echo the same concerns and willingness to guide. Myron Wakkuri of Elk Mountain Outfitters out of Wheatland has several thousand acres where he can hunt deer, elk, antelope, and bighorn sheep. He guided several clients with heart problems and fellows that were missing limbs. A lot of his hunts are conducted from four-by-fours. He said that each hunter and hunt would have to be evaluated individually. Another Wheatland outfitter guided a severely disabled but motivated hunter to a bighorn sheep near that town in September of 1993.

Kirk Atter has been inspired by his favorite sport for longer than he has been impaired. Kirk started hand-loading his own ammunition while a teenager in the 1960s. The 44-year old Buffalo, Wyoming man was struck with encephalitis in the early 1970s. Encephalitis is a nervous system disorder contracted from a virus. The virus caused inflammation of the brain and can cause permanent changes in the nervous system. A deterioration of intelligence, paralysis, disturbances of the heart, and breathing can all be results of the disease.

Kirk learned to deal with the ailment during the 1980s. By 1990, he had figured out how to hunt aggressively despite his balance problems, slow speech, and related disturbances of his nervous system. When he applied for a bighorn sheep permit, beat the stiff odds and drew, he knew that he must have backing for this hunt. He called Earnest Noble of Wheatland and booked a week-long hunt.

Noble is a new outfitter in the Wheatland area, who doubles as a schoolteacher and didn't mind helping Atter to his bighorn. Earnest had one of his guides help Kirk the first five days of September, when the season opened. Kenny concentrated their search in the central Laramie Mountains where Kirk saw about 20 sheep including three legal rams. He wasn't able to get close to them, partially due to his slowness. Kirk drove his truck back to Buffalo without a sheep, but he wasn't finished yet. Kirk nursed his depression, hoping for his outfitter to call him soon. He was proud of himself for negotiating nasty country on foot and horseback. He had to move slowly and he helped into the saddle, but he refused to let his disease stop him. He stayed close to the telephone just in case Noble should call. The outfitter's call came several days later.

"Kirk, why don't you get back down here," said the excited guide. "I think that we have a possibility."

Kirk hopped into his already loaded truck and steered it south on Interstate 25 to Wheatland. When he arrived, the outfitter had decided to guide Kirk personally. The Wyoming Game & Fish had transplanted a ram from near Esterbrook in the northern Laramie Mountains to a drainage further south. This ram had developed a protective instinct for hereford cows. I've learned from Game & Fish personnel that this practice among bighorn sheep isn't uncommon where sheep and domestic stock mix.

Now this ram was harassing bulls on a ranch near where he was moved to. The ranch foreman placed a concerned telephone call to the Game & Fish a few days earlier. The district game supervisor decided that this ram had to be harvested or he would be destroyed so he called Noble. As a result, Noble and Kirk set off into the Ashley Creek region on September 10th.

Noble had a good idea where the ram had last been seen. He had decided to abandon the horses, mainly because he felt they could cover more ground with a four-by-four. They split between glassing rocky hillsides and checking meadows along the creek. It was an anxious day. Noble had directions as to where the ram had been but there was a lot of country for a ram to hide in. They looked through binoculars until their eyes hurt. They drove from spot to spot, hoping to see the renegade ram, raising hell with the cattle. They had to search more openings before dusk overtook them that day. When they were slowly climbing a ridge that evening, Noble spotted something bedded down.

"There he is," he said excitedly, nudging Kirk. "He sure looks like the sheep I was told about."

"We can make a stalk along this slope," added Kirk, his eyes looking hungrily. "I bet we can get pretty close."

The pair took it slow along the uplift. Kirk couldn't move too fast and he didn't have to. Too many sportsmen are foiled in their haste to get from one place to another. Very soon, they had moved to within 50 yards, a cake-shot for someone with Kirk's experience. They thought it was cake until they wrestled to get Kirk in a prone position so that he could take the shot. Earnest and Kirk grappled to get Kirk's damaged body into the right position.

When the pair thought it was right, they waited for the ram to rise from his bed. Anxious minutes passed making Kirk decide to take him anyway. He was easily beyond the three-quarter minimum and legal. Kirk placed his .264 Winchester custom rifle on a bipod and drilled the outlaw through the shoulders, clipping his heart. Kirk would have liked to rush up to the fallen sheep, but he did the best that he could. When they arrived, the ram was dead, finished by Kirk's first shot.

The Game & Fish aged the ram at five years old and was nearly seven-eight curl. The ram was the only bighorn taken in the Laramie Range that year. Kirk had surely proven to himself that he could hunt aggressively, despite his handicap.

Helluva Hunt, 1562 Esterbrook Rd., Douglas, WY 82633 (307-358-6580). Wyoming Game & Fish, 5400 Bishop Blvd., Cheyenne, WY 82006-0001 (307-777-4600).

California

The state of California has been active in building handicapped access to waterfowl blinds in many of the refuges. The Imperial Wildlife Area has nine blinds for the handicapped. Grizzly Island, Mendoza Wildlife Area, and Delevan Refuge each have one blind apiece. Hunters with disabilities can qualify for a permit that allows them to shoot from the vehicle.

Contact the California Department Of Fish & Game for more information. Conservation Education Office, 1416 Ninth St., Sacramento, CA 95814 (916-653-6420

Colorado

Colorado is home to an outdoor group founded in 1986 by a retiree from Denver named Sid Sellers. Outdoor Buddies is an organization that pairs volunteers with mobility-handicapped sportspersons. Sid is the president of Outdoor Buddies, which has 15 people on its board of directors. Not only does Outdoor Buddies' focus on hunting but it helps disabled people enjoy fishing, canoeing, camping, and other outdoor activities.

Although first founded to help the mobility-disabled, Outdoor Buddies works with disabilities of all types and inner-city youth as well. For disabled individuals, it offers them a way of proving to themselves that it is still possible to rejoin the mainstream of life and enjoy a quality life standard. The organization offers them a way to enjoy activites that they thought were no longer available to them because of their hardships. For underprivileged youth, Outdoor Buddies provides an experience in life that they may have never known exisited. They no longer have to turn to drugs and gangs in order to find a degree of self-respect.

All types of hunting are purused by this non-profit organization. Outdoor Buddies searches for willing landowners who allow hunting, as well as volunteers who provide guide services. The club consists of 840 people, over half of whom are somehow impaired. Craig Hospital in Denver uses Outdoor Buddies as a rehabilitation tool. Craig has long been recognized as a major facility in the United States that specializes in rehabilitation. There are no fees for belonging to this group, spouses are always invited to particpate, and two events are held during each year. A dinner is held during February, and a picnic is staged in June. Locations used for hunting adventures are usually planned so that no interference can be expected from the general public.

Contact Outdoor Buddies, P.O. Box 37283, Denver, CO 80237 (303-771-8216).

Florida

Deer and feral hogs are hunted in Florida by Helluva Hunt, Southern Style by handicapped sportsmen using elevated stands. Morris Ingle of Green Grove got the idea of hunts for the handicapped when he participated in a similar hunt in nearby Georgia. Doves and bass fishing are other game sought after by this group of mostly Florida residents. The group will sometimes trade hunts so that disabled Floridians can hunt other states too. The association consists of 58 volunteers who help disabled hunters in their quest. Motels provide rooms and Winn-Dixie Supermarkets donates food for the events.

Helluva Hunt, Southern Style usually caters to 20 hunters annually, using hydraulic stands and ATVs to access their game.

Contact Helluva Hunt, Southern Style, 1619 Elsie St., Green Grove Springs, FL 32043 (904-284-2217).

Georgia

Georgia Handicapped Sportsmen, Inc. (G.H.S.) enables disabled sportsmen to pursue deer, turkey, dove, and also engage in bass fishing. One hundred thirty-five Georgia sportsmen belong to G.H.S. G.H.S. helps landowners thin large deer herds that are causing crop damage. These hunters chase game on private land, wildlife management areas, and Army Corps of Engineers property. Most of these hunters are mobility-disabled but a few are amputees or suffer other handicaps.

The club buys food, rents motel rooms, and gladly accepts donations. Paralyzed Veterans of America helps with these hunts and provides other support. Hunts take place from October through January or whenever seasons are open. They are based in Atlanta and are directed by Zeke Issak, a 67-year-old paraplegic from that state.

Contact Georgia Handicapped Sportsmen, Inc., 2138 Black Fox Dr., Atlanta, GA 30345 (404-636-3211).

Minnesota

Former outfitter Gary Stearns of Douglas, Wyoming motivated hunters from other states to provide disabled hunting services in their respective states. Daryl Rudquist and Douglas Bermel took the ball and got a similar hunt started in their state of Minnesota. The towns of Backus and Pine River are staging areas for Broken Wing Connection that provides pheasant hunting for the handicapped. The American Legion and Veterans of Foreign Wars provide support for these 20-bird hunts. Broken Wing Connection is more of a rehabilitative organization in that they desire to reach disabled hunters that have not been in the field.

Over 100 volunteers donate help for these bird hunts. Approximately 850 acres are used, including three hunting fields, archery ranges, trap facilities, and bird processing points. The club bears all expenses for the hunt except for transportation to the area. The hunts are scheduled for September as the normal pheasant season is later in the year when it is colder and hunters might experience difficulty or discomfort. About half of the hunters are Minnesota residents, while the remainder are from out of state. ATVs are used on the two-day hunts while a third day is reserved for organization and a banquet.

Contact Broken Wing Connection, HCR Box 105, Backus, MN 56435 (218-947-4307)

Nebraska

When the concept of outdoor recreation for the disabled was so successful in Colorado, Outdoor Buddies soon spread to surrounding states. They got their start in Nebraska in 1991 when Jerry Johnson started his own chapter in the town of North Platte. Johnson was hurt in a vehicle accident while ranching years earlier. Though disabled, Jerry didn't abandon his favorite sport and now helps others in the same predicament enjoy the outdoors. In Nebraska, Outdoor Buddies concentrates on hunting local game with an emphasis of birds. Nebraska has long been one of the premier upland game states in the country.

The organization also helps the disabled enjoy all other forms of outdoor recreation. Spouses are invited to participate. As in Colorado, Outdoor Buddies doesn't charge participants, believing the outdoors is a powerful rehabilitation tool.

Contact Outdoor Buddies, Box 37, Arnold, NE 69120 (308-848-2246) or 1815 S. 50th, Lincoln, NE 68506 (402-484-6504).

New Mexico

New Mexico offers a couple of elk hunts for hunters with disabilities. These hunts are offered on a drawing basis. One takes place in the Gila National Forest (50 hunters) and the other occurs in the Lincoln National Forest (30 hunters). The odds of drawing the hunts are good. Many state guides are equipped to handle disabled hunters.

Contact New Mexico Game & Fish Department, Box 25112, Villagra Bldg., Santa Fe, NM 87504 (505-827-7911).

Here are how eight different states help unfortunate hunters enjoy the outdoors. Hunting is the main activity of these organizations. Groups exist all over the country to help disabled or disease victims continue their love of an ancient sport. State wildlife agencies should have information about these organizations. All of these clubs need able volunteers to help impaired hunters pursue their game. Landowners can help by providing access for disabled hunters. Where there's a will, here's the way. These groups help impaired hunters pursue wildlife again and enjoy life.

Participants in Wyoming Helluva Hunt enjoy trap-shooting, antelope hunting, a barbecue, and a dinner in Douglas, Wyoming.

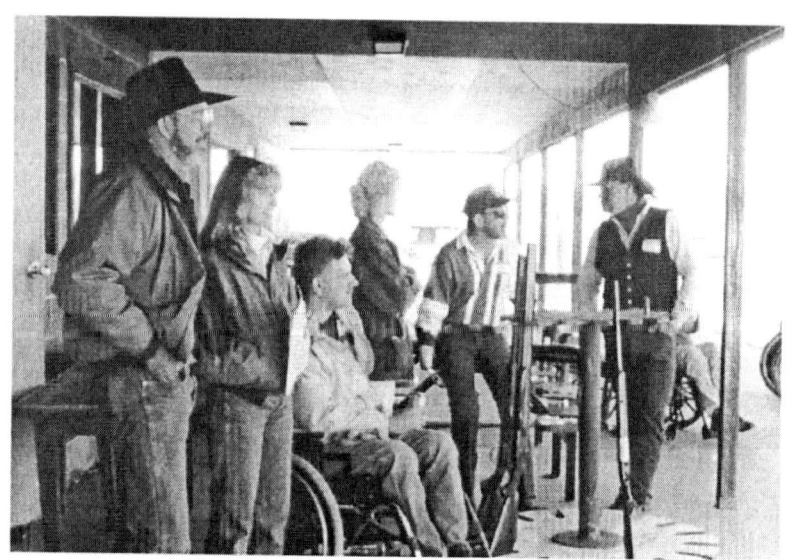

Started in Wyoming by former outfitter Gary Stearns and his wife Janet (left), Helluva Hunt has spread to several states throughout the nation. Participants enjoy trap-shooting at the event.

Helluva Hunt (Wyoming) assists many disabled sportsmen in hunting antelope every year. Volunteers help a blind hunter sight his rifle.

Wyoming Helluva Hunt's Gary Stearns assists a visually impaired hunter sight-in his rifle. Helluva Hunt acquires permission for disabled sportsmen to hunt antelope each year near Douglas, Wyoming.

Kirk Atter with a Yellowstone elk he killed on a late-season migration hunt near Jackson, Wyoming.

Volunteers at Wyoming Helluva Hunt watch a quadriplegic participant sight-in his rifle. The trigger was tripped by this gentleman's mouth.

Kirk harvested a cattle-harassing Wyoming Bighorn Sheep in 1986 near Wheatland, Wyoming.

Encephalitis didn't stop Kirk Atter from harvesting a record book Alaskan caribou.

Boone & Crockett Caribou are certainly something to smile about, especially for Kirk.

Afterword

Fortitude drove these men to recover and to accept the disability that beset them. Their drive to enjoy a sport that they once excelled in was a moderating factor in negotiating the hardships that they faced. They all have an intense love of hunting. There is a growing anti-hunting or animal-rights sentiment in the United States today. Here is an example of how this powerful sport allowed some handicapped individuals to battle their impediment. In some cases, hunting actually helped an individual recover. In all instances, the sport allowed these hunters a release from the beds, pain, boredom, and limited world they had become resigned to.

Each disability has profound intrusions in the lives of these hunters. Jim has constant pain; Pat and Jerry will probably never walk again, and Roy will never see things like a normal person does. Ken is always haunted by the uncertainty of another heart-attack. Kirk is never going to win a debate and I may never be able to think coherently again. We are all the same though, in our struggle and our love for hunting. Jerry promotes the sport in his native Nebraska. Jim invites other hunters to enjoy the bird-hunting that he loves. Roy is active in shooting sports in Laramie. And I write about my favorite sport as long as there is no deadline pressure to unsettle me.

All of these men have been compensated for their loss in some way. None of us would care to follow the same path again, no matter what hunting we now enjoy. We would all much rather have our lives back to normal so we could do things like we once could. But that is not going to be, so we must all either roll with the punch or choose not to hunt. After the way we were all raised, not hunting isn't an option. So we adapt, compensate, adjust, and fandangle our way back into the sport. We all speak a common language that has been tempered by both physical and mental pain. We are all more compassionate, though hardened. All seven of us have lived more years than the Creator puts in a man's lifetime. We are all blessed with people that love us, understand, and are committed to helping us lead normal lives. Many times in a week, I am not able to function normally. My wife or parents give me distance, push me, or take up the slack, accordingly.

Every one of these hunters that I've written about has someone that is committed to helping them through their plight. The family is often the best weapon you can have to handle a problem. You don't have to be in a wheelchair to be disabled. We all harbor problems that have tried their best to knock us out. If some people don't understand, there are a lot more compassionate folks that do. And there is a lot more hunting to be done.